Illustrated

ATLAS
of Ancient
EGYPT

Delia Pemberton

THE BRITISH MUSEUM PRESS

First published in 2005 by British Museum Press
A division of The British Museum Company Ltd
46 Bloomsbury Street, London WC1B 3QQ

www.britishmuseum.co.uk

A catalogue record for this title is available from the British Library

ISBN-13: 978-0-7141-3008-8
ISBN-10: 0-7141-3008-7

Designed and typeset by Ewing Paddock
Printed in China by C & C Offset

Author's acknowledgements

A big thank-you to everyone involved in the production of this book, especially my friends and colleagues at the British Museum and British Museum Press, too numerous to name individually, who gave so generously of their time and expertise. Special thanks are due to my ever-wonderful editor Carolyn Jones, to the book designer Ewing Paddock, to Beatriz Waters (probably the hardest-working picture researcher in the world) and to Richard Parkinson and Neal Spencer for their many helpful suggestions. A big hand, too, for my support team, headed up by Paul Strange, who put up with me while I was writing it. Intermittent feline companionship was provided by Mr Mars of Kingston.

Dedication
This book is dedicated to Anne and Dan: 'Buy one, get two free'

Illustration acknowledgements

Photographs are taken by the British Museum Photography and Imaging Dept, © The Trustees of the British Museum, unless otherwise stated below.

Maps by ML Design

Ashmolean Museum, University of Oxford: 41 bottom left

John Baines: 20 top

Christine Barrett: drawing on 74

BFI Stills, Posters and Designs/Courtesy of Universal Studios Licensing LLLP: 10 bottom

© Bildarchiv Preussischer Kulturbesitz, Berlin, Agyptisches Museum und Papyrussammlung. Photograph: Margarete Bussing: 59 top left

Bridgeman Art Library: 88 top
Louvre, Paris, France, Lauros/Giraudon/ Bridgeman Art Library: 89 bottom right
Private collection, Lauros/Giraudon/ Bridgeman Art Library: 88 bottom left
Scottish National Portrait Gallery, Edinburgh, Scotland/Bridgeman Art Library: 88 bottom right

Corbis:
© Bettman/Corbis: 91 top left
© Richard T. Nowitz/Corbis: 75 bottom left
© Gianni Dagli Orti/Corbis: 90 centre
© Ron Watts/Corbis: 87 centre left

Éditions Errance: 42 bottom right, 46 centre, 49 top, 50 top, 58 bottom, 60 top, 65 bottom, 69 top, 77 top, 84 bottom right

Courtesy of the Egypt Exploration Society/Photograph © P.T. Nicholson: 47 top right

Joyce Filer: 90 top, 93 centre right, 93 bottom left

Fitzwilliam Museum, Cambridge: 80 bottom left

Werner Forman Archive: 35 bottom right, 48 centre, 50 bottom right, 67 centre right (photo E. Strouhal), 75 bottom right (Werner Forman/Egyptian Museum, Cairo)

Geoed Ltd: 10 centre

The Griffith Institute, Ashmolean Museum, Oxford: 75 top right, 75 centre (drawn by H. Parkinson)

Graham Harrison: 6 top, 6 bottom, 7, 12 top, 13 bottom left, 20 centre, 21 centre left, 27 bottom, 31 top, 34 bottom left, 38 centre, 40 top left, 40 top centre, 48 top, 48 bottom left, 54 top, 54 centre, 55 centre, 56-7 bottom, 61 bottom, 66 top, 67 bottom left, 71 top right, 76 top, 83 bottom, 84 top right, 86 top, 86 centre left, 87 top right, 90 bottom, 91 bottom left

National Museums Liverpool: 80 centre

NASA/Science Photo Library: 13 top left

© The Natural History Museum, London: 10 top centre, 22 bottom right, 55 bottom right

NHPA/Photograph: Nigel J. Dennis: 57 centre right
NHPA/Photograph: Brian Hawkes: 21 centre right
NHPA/Photograph: Karl Switak: 86 centre right

Paul T. Nicholson: 32 bottom, 35 top right, 39 bottom, 50 bottom left, 79 bottom left, 84 bottom left

Lorna Oakes: 85 top

© Richard Parkinson: 34 bottom right, 42 bottom left, 69 centre, 70 bottom, 79 bottom right

Delia Pemberton: 13 top right, 16 top, 17 bottom right, 18 top, 18 bottom, 19, 22 top left, 31 centre right, 33 bottom, 36 top, 37 bottom right, 38 top, 40 centre bottom, 40 top right, 41 top left, 41 centre, 41 top right, 46 top right, 47 centre, 47 bottom, 48 bottom right, 49 bottom, 51 centre right, 51 bottom right, 61 top right, 62 bottom right, 62 top, 63 top right, 63 bottom left, 65 top right, 68 bottom, 70 top, 70 centre left, 70 centre right, 74 top, 76 centre right, 78 bottom, 79 top left, 79 top right, 81 top left, 81 top right, 81 bottom, 82 top, 83 top right, 85 bottom left, 91 bottom right, 92 bottom left

Petrie Museum of Egyptian Archaeology, University College London UC.7196: 51 bottom left

© Red-Head: 68 top

© Photo RMN – Chuzeville: 41 bottom right
© Photo RMN – Michèle Bellot: 92 top

Philip Sayer: 93 bottom right

William Schenck: drawings on 46, 77

Science Museum/Science & Society Picture Library: 22 bottom right

Ian Shaw: 82 bottom

Alan Sorrell, R.W.S., pen ink and wash drawing of Semna fortress, 26 centre

Nigel Strudwick: typesetting of hieroglyphs on p. 20.

Claire Thorne: drawings on 11 bottom, 45 left, 48, 62 centre, 81 centre left

UNESCO: 93 centre left

Contents

What fascinates you about ancient Egypt?

Mummies? Pyramids? Pharaohs? Golden treasures? Hieroglyphs? Everyone has some favourite thing which they associate with Egypt. But have you ever wondered where the ancient Egyptians came from and why their civilization developed the way it did?

One of the first western tourists to ancient Egypt, the Greek historian Herodotus, called Egypt 'the gift of the river'. He realized that without the River Nile people would never have been able to live in Egypt.

Right: King Thutmose III.
Below: King Rameses II receiving tribute of African produce.

The Nile shaped the lives and beliefs of the ancient Egyptians in many important ways, from the food they ate and the clothes they wore to their society and religion. For the first Egyptians, the Nile provided fish to catch, birds and animals to hunt and wild plants to gather. It was also the highway that allowed them to travel and trade with people in other countries. Later, they learned to use the rich black earth along the Nile's banks to grow crops, make pots and build houses.

But Egypt's deserts were important, too. They protected Egypt by making it difficult for enemies to invade. Although they were wild and dangerous, the deserts were rich in natural

NCIENT EGYPT!

resources. Hidden in the desert mountains were sources of gold and gemstones that helped make Egypt rich and powerful. The mountains were also the source of the stones the Ancient Egyptians used for buildings, and of the ores used to produce metals from which tools and weapons were made. Most importantly, the desert was where the great sun god rose each morning and set each evening.

Everything in ancient Egypt was connected to the natural world – plants and animals, gods and goddesses, people and cities, work and leisure, politics and warfare. With the help of the *Illustrated Atlas of Ancient Egypt*, you too can enter the world of the ancient Egyptians.

HOW TO USE THE ATLAS

The *Atlas* is divided into the following four main sections.

- **Part one, Introduction to Ancient Egypt**, gives background information about Egypt's history and geography.

- **Part two, The Ancient Egyptian World**, explains how Egypt was formed and how the Egyptian environment shaped the development of ancient Egypt.

- **Part three, Places, Customs and Beliefs**, contains the maps and descriptions of the Nile Delta, the Nile Valley, and the

Deserts and Oases as they were from about 5000 BC to the end of the Roman Period (AD 395). Also, there are Spotlights on important places and features on aspects of ancient Egyptian life and beliefs.

- **Part four, The Study of Egypt**, looks at the recent history of Egypt, and tells how the secrets of ancient Egypt are being uncovered.

The *Atlas* also has a Glossary explaining unfamiliar words, a list of other books on ancient Egypt which you might like to read, and an Index.

Have fun exploring ancient Egypt!

PART ONE
INTRODUCTION TO
ANCIENT EGYPT
MODERN EGYPT

Egypt is a country on the north-eastern coast of Africa, bordered by the Mediterranean Sea to the north, the Red Sea to the east and the Sahara Desert to the south and west. The Mediterranean and the Red Sea are connected by the Suez Canal. Today, Egypt's neighbours are Libya in the west, Israel in the east and Sudan in the south. In ancient times, political frontiers in the region were always changing, as rival kingdoms gained and lost territory.

Modern Egypt covers an area of just over a million square kilometres (386,000 square miles), about the same amount of land that the ancient Egyptians controlled at the height of their power. However, today there is a much bigger population. Over 60 million people now live in Egypt – at least ten times as many as in ancient times. The capital and biggest city is Cairo, with a population of more than 7 million.

Just like their ancestors, modern Egyptian farmers use cattle to plough their fields.

Modern Cairo.

Egypt can be divided into four main regions: the River Nile, the Western Desert (also called the Libyan Desert) to the west of the Nile, the Eastern Desert (also called the Arabian Desert) to the east of the Nile, and the Sinai Peninsula. Looking at the maps of Egypt in this book, you can see that most of the country is desert. Because of this, most Egyptians have always preferred to live on the fertile land along the Nile.

One reason why the Nile is so important is that Egypt's climate is very hot and dry. Rain is rare, and the daytime temperature in the desert can be as high as 50°C. Apart from the desert oases and some underground springs, all of Egypt's water for drinking and growing food comes from the Nile.

The River Nile runs the whole length of Egypt, from the south to the north, a distance of over 1500 km (930 miles). In ancient times, the Nile overflowed each summer, covering the river banks with soil that piled up to form a fertile floodplain. Today, the flood waters are held back by the Aswan High Dam in southern Egypt, creating a lake that stretches south into Sudan. This lake is named Lake Nasser, after the first president of modern Egypt. The water stored in Lake Nasser is released gradually through the year when it is needed, so that more land can be used to grow food.

In southern Egypt, the Nile Valley is very narrow, usually measuring no more than 3 km (nearly 2 miles) across. Further north it gets wider

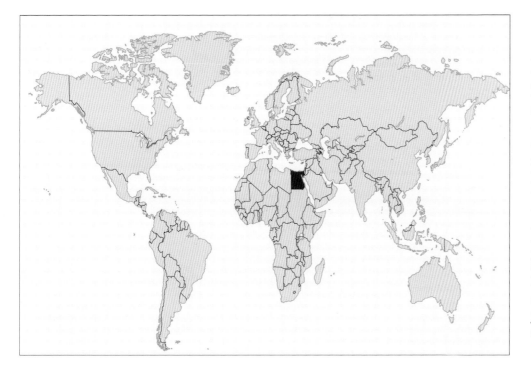

Modern Egypt.

as the river slows down on its way to the sea. Just north of Cairo, the Nile spreads out to create a fan-shaped delta covering an area of about 15,000 square kilometres (5,800 square miles). Although the fertile land of the Nile Valley and Delta makes up only 4% of Egypt's total area, 96% of its population live there. Most of the others live along the Suez Canal and in the oases. Even though there are now several big cities such as Cairo, most Egyptians still live in the countryside and work as farmers, just as they have done for thousands of years.

Market day in modern Cairo.

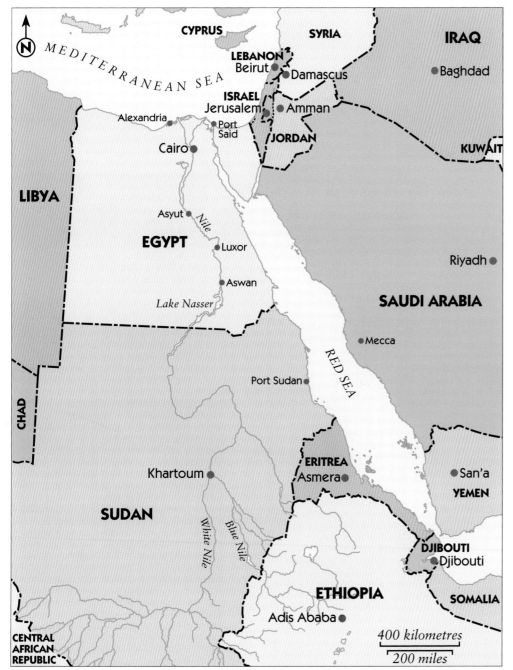

Egypt factfile

Area	1,001,450 sq km
Fertile land	5%
Desert	95%
Climate	Hot, dry
Average temperatures (Cairo)	
Summer	20-36°C
Winter	10-20°C
Rainfall	Less than 80mm a year
Population in 2001	69,536,644
Government	Republic
Language	Arabic

EGYPT AND ITS HISTORY

Until Egyptologists learned to read ancient Egyptian scripts in the 1820s, people got their ideas about ancient Egyptian history from the Bible and from books written by early Greek and Roman historians. An early history of Egypt was written around 300 BC by an Egyptian priest called Manetho, and the way in which Egyptian history is described today is based on the system he used.

Manetho divided Egypt's rulers into 30 *Dynasties* or families. Later, Egyptologists grouped these dynasties into periods called *Kingdoms*. There are three kingdoms – the Old Kingdom, the Middle Kingdom and the New Kingdom. These kingdoms were times when Egypt was united under one ruler. In between the kingdoms were times now known as *Intermediate Periods*, when Egypt was divided into two or

Prehistoric Period
c. 100,000 – c. 5500 BC

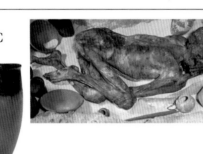

▼

Predynastic Period
c. 5500 – c. 3100 BC

▼

Early Dynastic Period
c. 3100 – c. 2686 BC
1st and 2nd Dynasties

▼

Old Kingdom
c. 2686 – c. 2181 BC
3rd-6th Dynasties

▼

1st Intermediate Period
c. 2181 – c. 2055 BC

▼

Middle Kingdom
c. 2055 – c. 1650 BC
11th-14th Dynasties

▼

2nd Intermediate Period
c. 1650 – c. 1550 BC
15th-17th Dynasties

▼

New Kingdom
c. 1550 – c. 1069 BC
18th-20th Dynasties

▼

3rd Intermediate Period
c. 1069 – c. 747 BC
21st-24th Dynasties

▼

more territories with different rulers. There are three of these: the First Intermediate Period, the Second Intermediate Period and the Third Intermediate Period.

The Kingdoms and Intermediate Periods do not cover all of ancient Egyptian history. Prehistoric times in Egypt are called the *Predynastic Period* because they come before the dynasties of kings. The reigns of Egypt's very first kings are grouped together as the *Early Dynastic Period*. The time after the Third Intermediate Period, when the rule of Egypt kept changing hands between Egyptians and foreigners, is called the *Late Period*. After Alexander the Great conquered Egypt in the 4th century BC, it was ruled by a Greek family called the Ptolemies. Their rulership is called the *Ptolemaic Period*.

Eventually, the Ptolemies were defeated by the Romans, and Egypt became a part of the Roman Empire. This is the *Roman Period*. In the 4th century AD, the Roman Empire divided and Egypt became part of the Christian Byzantine Empire. This is the called the *Byzantine Period*. In the 7th century AD, the Byzantine rulers of Egypt were driven out by the Arabs, who established an Islamic state that had many different rulers over the centuries. Egypt became a republic in 1952.

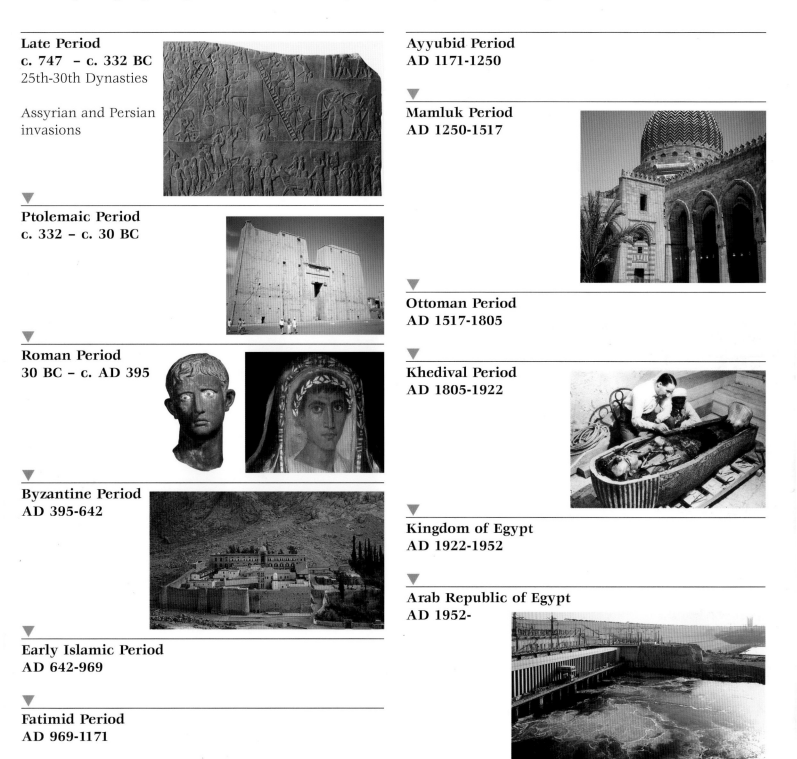

Late Period
c. 747 – c. 332 BC
25th-30th Dynasties

Assyrian and Persian invasions

Ptolemaic Period
c. 332 – c. 30 BC

Roman Period
30 BC – c. AD 395

Byzantine Period
AD 395-642

Early Islamic Period
AD 642-969

Fatimid Period
AD 969-1171

Ayyubid Period
AD 1171-1250

Mamluk Period
AD 1250-1517

Ottoman Period
AD 1517-1805

Khedival Period
AD 1805-1922

Kingdom of Egypt
AD 1922-1952

Arab Republic of Egypt
AD 1952-

PART TWO
THE ANCIENT
EGYPTIAN WORLD
THE
GEOLOGY
OF EGYPT

Fossilized wood from Egypt.

Until about 50 million years ago, most of Egypt was underneath the sea. The plants and animals living in the sea produced carbon dioxide, which caused carboniferous rocks, such as limestone, to form on the sea-bed. As the plants and animals died, their bodies drifted down to become part of the sea-bed as fossils.

On land, the rocks that had formed the original surface of the earth were continually being worn away by the action of the wind and rain. When the animals and plants that lived on the land died, their bodies decomposed and mixed with the fragments of the eroded rock to form soil and sedimentary rock. Some animals and plants were preserved as fossils, and these help us to understand the way in which Egypt's land and climate changed in prehistoric times.

Ever since its formation, the earth has kept changing. In some places,

Above: Limestone with fossil sea creatures (nummulites).

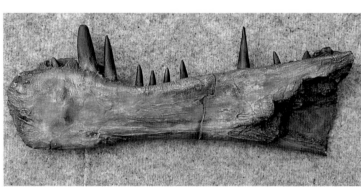

Left: The fossilized jaw of a spinosaurus.

the sea-bed has been pushed up to form mountain ranges. In other places, dry land has sunk under the sea. The earth's crust has been pushed and pulled apart to form the continents. Even today, the earth's

Spinosaurus aegypticus lived in Bahariya oasis about 95 million years ago. It was a fearsome predator. Even a young spinosaurus measured 15 m (49 ft) long and weighed between 9 and 15 tons.

movement is sometimes strong enough for us to experience it as an earthquake.

In the northern part of Egypt, the sea-bed was pushed up to form limestone mountains, which is why today this area is made of limestone. The southern part of Egypt, which was not under the sea, is made of sandstone. In the very south, hard rocks such as granite, which formed the earth's original surface, can sometimes be seen pushing out through the sandstone. The rocks from which Egypt is made can readily be seen because they have been exposed by the action of wind and rain, and especially by the River Nile. Over millions of years, the river wore away the rocks to create a deep valley. Today, the Nile is the longest river in the world, but it began as just one of many rivers carrying water northwards from the heart of Africa to the Mediterranean Sea. Over time, some of these rivers began to flow together until they were strong enough to wear away the softest parts of the rocks that form Egypt. As the new river became deeper, more water flowed into it, cutting a deeper and deeper course through the sandstone of southern Egypt and the limestone of northern Egypt to create the Nile Valley.

But the water could not cut through the hard rocks underneath. In the far south of Egypt, the hard granite sometimes comes to the surface, interrupting the flow of the river. These interruptions are called *cataracts*.

As it slows down on its way to the sea, the Nile spreads out and splits into different branches, creating a huge, flat triangular area of fertile land. Geographers call this kind of river plain a *delta*, because it looks like the Greek capital letter delta (Δ). In ancient times, there were at least seven main branches of the Nile in the Delta, but today there are just two.

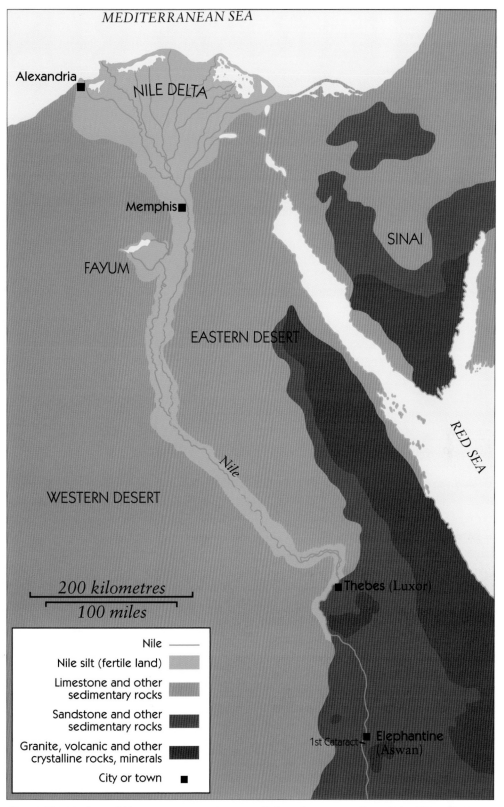

Above: The geology of Egypt.

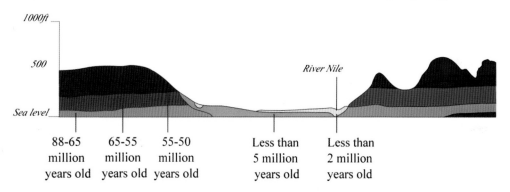

Below: A cross section of the Nile valley south of Thebes showing its geology.

THE RIVER NILE

In the 19th century, explorers began tracking the routes of Africa's great rivers. Until then, nobody knew where the Nile came from. The ancient Egyptians believed that it flowed from a cave underneath the First Nile Cataract, where the town of Aswan is today. Now we know that the Nile has two main sources, the White Nile and the Blue Nile, which join at Khartoum in modern Sudan.

The White Nile and the Blue Nile are quite different from each other. The White Nile begins in Lake Victoria Nyanza, which lies between Uganda, Tanzania and Kenya. Its waters flow steadily throughout the year. The Blue Nile is made up of many small streams which flow together to carry away the rainwater which falls on the Ethiopian highlands every winter. For most of the year, the Blue Nile is quite low, but in the spring it begins to swell as it fills up with water and soil washed down by the rain.

In ancient times, this floodwater reached the Nile Valley in summer and made the river overflow. The water spread out across the valley bottom, leaving behind the soil it carried. Over millions of years, this soil piled up to make Egypt's fertile floodplain. Because this fertile earth was so precious to them, the ancient Egyptians called their country *Kemet*, which means the Black Land. The desert, where nothing could grow, was called *Deshret*, the Red Land.

The ancient Egyptians were completely dependent on the Nile for its fertile silt and life-giving water. They became expert at managing the Nile flood by directing the water into reservoirs, where it could be stored and distributed to the fields via networks of channels. Every field had its own channels, so the farmer could direct the precious water exactly where it was needed.

Ancient Egyptians believed the god Hapy poured the Nile waters out from his cave in the First Nile cataract.

Satellite photograph of Egypt.

Egypt's rich farmland was created by the River Nile.

To raise the water from the channels into the fields, farmers used a water scoop called a *shaduf*. The shaduf is a long pole with a bucket at one end and a heavy weight at the other. The pole is balanced on a frame so that when the empty bucket is let down into the water, the weight can be tipped down to lift up the full bucket. Moving water with a shaduf is very slow, and hard work, and in later times waterwheels worked by donkeys or oxen were used instead.

A shaduf beside the Nile.

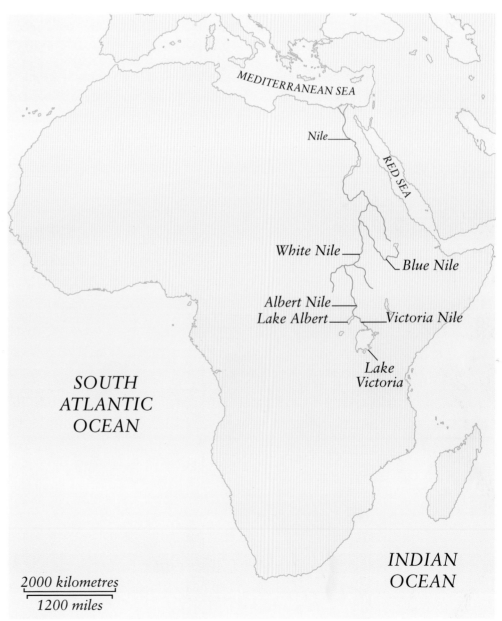

MEDITERRANEAN SEA

RED SEA

Nile

White Nile

Blue Nile

Albert Nile

Lake Albert

Victoria Nile

Lake Victoria

SOUTH ATLANTIC OCEAN

INDIAN OCEAN

2000 kilometres

1200 miles

The sources of the Nile.

THE FIRST EGYPTIANS

Today, Egypt is very hot and dry, but it was not always like that. About 1.7 million years ago, huge ice sheets covered all of northern Europe. Because this polar ice came so much further south than it does today, north Africa was much cooler. What are now Egypt's deserts were once forests and plains where animals such as gazelles, giraffes and ostriches roamed.

Human life began in Africa, and by 100,000 years ago, Stone Age people were already living in Egypt. Gathered in big family groups called clans, they travelled the plains hunting, fishing and collecting edible plants and berries. They made their weapons and tools from stone and bones, and wore clothes of animal skins.

A stone knife blade made by prehistoric Egyptians around 100,000 BC.

But about 20,000 years ago, the climate in Egypt began to change. The polar ice was melting, and the weather became warmer. Rain fell less often, and the grasslands and forests began to dry up and disappear. By about 5,000 years ago, the only places left with water and vegetation were the Nile Valley, the Delta and the desert oases, where spring water rises to the surface, creating areas of fertile land.

So, the families of hunters began living in these places, where they could still find animals and birds to hunt, fish to catch and plants to gather. Since they could find everything they needed in one place, they stopped travelling so much, and started to build houses of mud and reeds. Instead of always hunting animals, they learned to tame and breed them. Cattle, sheep and goats were kept for their meat and milk, ducks, geese and pigeons for their meat, bees for their honey, and donkeys for carrying heavy loads.

The settlers also discovered that they could grow more of the plants which they liked to eat by taking their seeds and scattering them on the fresh, wet earth left behind each year by the Nile flood. Some cereals, such as wheat and barley, had to be cooked to make them edible, and hence the Egyptians learned to make them into bread and beer. For most of Egyptian history, bread and beer was the main diet. People still lived in clans, but their villages were growing larger. Because they were not constantly moving on, the villagers had more time to make things from the natural materials

Early hunters used bows and arrows, spears, clubs and throwing sticks. Their prey included lions, gazelles and ostriches.

Basket from the Fayum, made about 5000 BC.

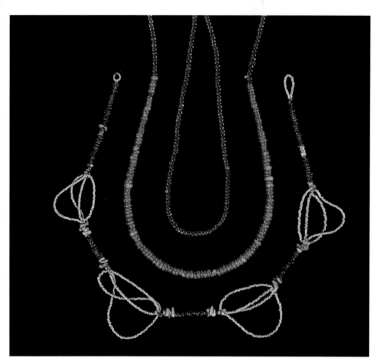

Gold and gemstone jewellery, made about 3000 BC.

Model cattle from a tomb, made about 3500 BC.

which they found around them. They learned to make pots from the Nile mud, baskets from reeds and palm leaves, and cloth from plant fibres. Some people began to specialize in making these things. If they made more than they needed for themselves, they could exchange them with their neighbours for other things they wanted.

Farmers found that they could grow more food if they kept back the Nile floodwaters to water their fields, and they became experts at building dams, canals and reservoirs to control the water. A farmer could not do these things on his own; all the farmers in the community had to work together and to help each other. There had to be rules about how much water each farmer could use, and when he could use it.

Neighbouring clans were not always friendly. Often, there were fights between them over the ownership of land, water and other resources. After a while, people realised that it was better for everyone to cooperate with their neighbours. As local communities grew bigger, people found

they needed laws to make sure that resources were distributed fairly, and community leaders to make sure that the laws were obeyed. This was the beginning of government in Egypt.

Pottery jar, made about 4000 BC.

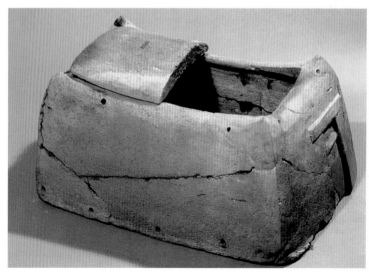

Pottery model house from about 3200 BC.

GODS AND GODDES

As the Egyptians explored their environment, they wondered where everything came from, and looked for ways to explain how nature worked. All around them, they saw gods and goddesses in the mountains and the river, in birds, animals and insects, in plants and trees, in the earth and sky, and in the sun, stars and moon. All the forces of nature, fierce and gentle, were represented by Egypt's gods and goddesses. The clever baboon became Thoth, the god of learning. The jackal who prowled the cemeteries became Anubis, the god of mummification. The motherly cow became Hathor, the goddess of love and fertility.

People looked at the sun and the Nile, and invented stories of how the world was created by a sun god who came out of the water. First the sun god created Shu, the god of air, and Tefnut, the goddess of moisture. Then came Geb, the earth god, and Nut, the sky goddess. Geb and Nut had four children – the gods Osiris and Seth, and the goddesses Isis and Nephthys.

After the sun god had created everything, he was tired. He put Osiris and Seth in charge of Egypt. But while Osiris' half flourished and became the Black Land, Seth's half turned into the desert, the Red Land.

The god Ra as a falcon wearing the sun disk and sacred cobra as a headdress.

Seth was jealous and murdered Osiris, but Osiris' wife, his sister Isis, made sure that their son Horus became king in his place. Osiris could not return to life on earth, but he did live again as the ruler of the Underworld, the land of the dead.

The Egyptians thought that the entrance to the Underworld was in the western horizon, where the sun set each evening. They believed the sun god was born every morning as

The air god, Shu, raises the goddess Nut to create the sky. Geb lies on the ground below.

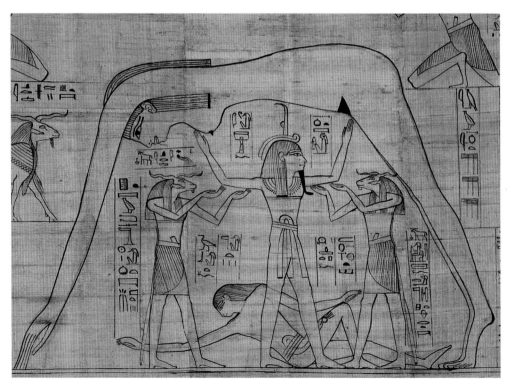

The jackal-headed god Anubis.

The goddess Isis and her son Horus.

Osiris, worshipped as the god of the dead.

the god Khephri. At midday, he was called Ra, and in the afternoon, Atum. In the evening, he died and entered the Underworld. After travelling through the Underworld during the night hours, he was born again the next morning. In one version of this story, the setting sun was swallowed each evening by the sky goddess Nut, passed through her body and was reborn each morning.

From watching these cycles of nature, the Egyptians developed

The god Thoth shown as a baboon.

their ways of thinking about life and death. They hoped that, like Osiris, they would have another life after they died. They put their cemeteries in deserts to the west of their towns in order that the dead could follow the sun into the Underworld. They also made sure that the graves contained everything people would need for the next life.

All life in Egypt depended on the Nile flood. When there was too little water, the crops could not grow.

The temple of Isis at Philae.

When there was too much water, fields, houses and animals would be washed away. Either way, the people would starve. The Egyptians believed that their gods and goddesses could make sure that everything in life and nature stayed in balance. The government made images of these deities and built temples for them to live in. Priests and priestesses were appointed to act as their servants. They prayed to the gods and goddesses on behalf of the community, and made offerings to the divine images in the hope of winning their favour.

THE KING

The most important person in ancient Egypt was the king. In prehistoric times, there were no kings of Egypt, only clan leaders and local chieftains. But some time around 3100 BC, a warrior chief from the south conquered the Nile Delta and became the first ruler of all Egypt. According to ancient legends, this king was called Menes, but this might be another name for a real king called Narmer. Narmer's greatest achievement was to unite the Nile Valley and the Nile Delta, the Two Lands of Upper Egypt and Lower Egypt. To mark this unification, he founded Egypt's first capital city, Memphis, close to where the Nile Valley joins the Delta (see page 32).

After this time, kings of Egypt were given titles like Lord of the Two Lands and King of Upper and Lower Egypt. From the New Kingdom (1550-1069 BC) onwards, the king was sometimes called *Pharaoh*. This term means 'great house', and referred originally to a royal court or palace.

The ancient Egyptians believed that every king was the son of the gods. It was the king's responsibility to maintain the balance of nature so that Egypt would flourish, just as it had flourished under Osiris at the beginning of time. Because the king was a god himself, he could speak to the other gods and goddesses on behalf of his people. In every temple of Egypt, paintings and carvings showed him making offerings to the gods and goddesses to make sure of their help.

Egyptian society was like a pyramid, with the king at the top. Underneath him were his high officials and the local governors who ruled Egypt's provinces. Below them were the civil servants, temple priests and landowners. Next, came the skilled craftspeople and traders, and finally, at the bottom, the peasants who farmed the land.

King Ptolemy VIII receives the Double Crown of Upper and Lower Egypt from the goddesses of the Nile Delta and the Nile Valley.

Officials counting geese for taxation.

Nile gods tie lotus and papyrus plants together to symbolize the union of the Nile Valley and the Delta.

Egypt was divided into 42 provinces, called *nomes*. There were 22 nomes in the Nile Valley and 20 in the Nile Delta. Each nome was ruled by a governor, whose job was to keep the peace, to maintain the network of canals which watered the fields, and to collect the taxes which went to the government.

Maat was the Egyptian goddess of divine order. By offering a figure of Maat to the gods, kings showed they were upholding order in Egypt.

The Egyptians did not use money until Ptolemaic times. Instead, they traded work or produce for the goods and services they needed. This system is called *bartering*. So, taxes were not paid in money, but in goods or labour. Every two years, the tax officials travelled the country, making sure that everyone paid their dues to the government. Farmers had to give a share of their crops and livestock, craftsmen a share of what they had made, labourers a share of their working time.

These taxes were used to pay government employees, to build temples and royal monuments, to fund trading and mining expeditions, to maintain the army, and to make offerings to the gods and goddesses. All these expenses, and many more, were administered by the army of scribes who made up the king's civil service.

The scribes dated their documents with the year number of the reigning king. This showed how many years he had been on the throne. When a king died, they started again with Year 1 of the new king.

NOME SIGNS

Nome boundary ....
Nome numbers:
   Upper Egypt   **9**
   Lower Egypt   **13**

The nomes (provinces) of ancient Egypt.

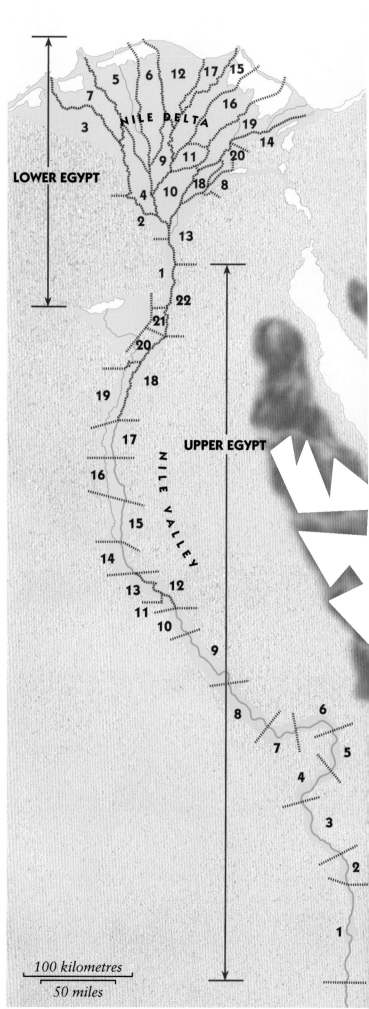

100 kilometres
50 miles

THE EGYPTIAN YEAR

The ancient Egyptians based their calendar on observation of the sun, the moon and the stars. Their day was measured by the rising and setting of the sun, their month by the waxing and waning of the moon, and their year by the return of the Nile flood. They learned to tell when the flood would come by watching the rising of the bright Dog Star Sirius in the night sky.

These hieroglyphs say:
'Year 28 under the person of the king of Upper and Lower Egypt Nimaatra (Amenemhat III) living forever'.

Above: During the Nile inundation, Egypt's farmland was completely flooded.

Below: Tomb painting of farm workers winnowing grain to remove the husks.

The Nile flood marked the start of the Egyptian year, which contained 360 days, plus five extra days sacred to the gods. The 360 days of the year were divided into 12 months of 30 days each, and each month into three 10-day weeks. There were three seasons, each lasting four months, which followed the pattern of the farming year. The seasons were called *Akhet* (inundation), *Peret* (growing) and *Shemu* (harvest). They mirrored the story of Osiris, who, just like the crops, had been killed and buried but rose again.

Akhet, the first season of the year, began in summer, when the Nile flooded the fields. Channels directed the floodwater into reservoirs, which were dammed to hold back the water for irrigating the fields. As the floodwater went down, Peret began. This was the season when the crops were planted and grew.

Farmers ploughed and hoed the soil, scattered seed and drove herds of animals over the fields to press the seeds into the earth.

As the crops grew, the farmers tended them, pulling up weeds and chasing off birds and other pests that tried to eat the crops. Water from the reservoirs was directed into a network of channels to irrigate the fields.

A wooden tomb model of a farmer ploughing.

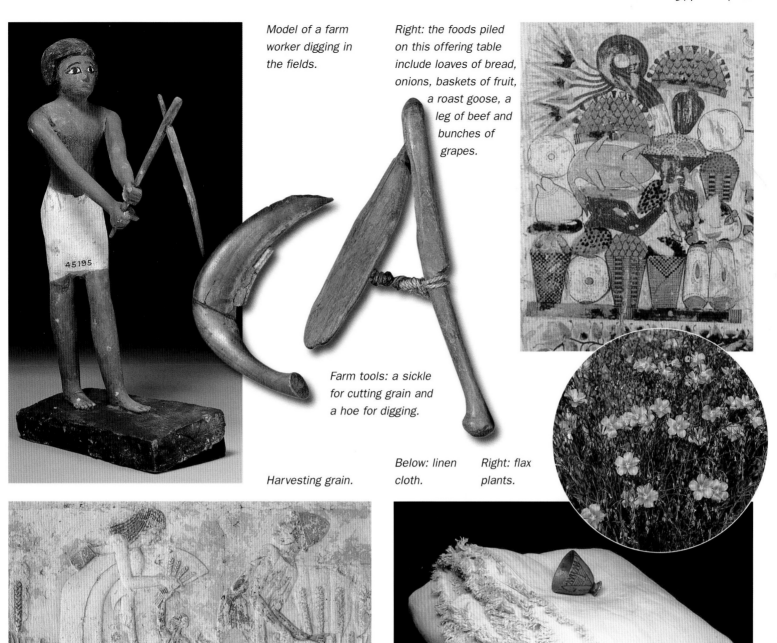

Model of a farm worker digging in the fields.

Right: the foods piled on this offering table include loaves of bread, onions, baskets of fruit, a roast goose, a leg of beef and bunches of grapes.

Farm tools: a sickle for cutting grain and a hoe for digging.

Harvesting grain.

Below: linen cloth.

Right: flax plants.

During Shemu, the fields of Egypt filled with workers as everyone who could helped to harvest the crops. Wheat and barley were threshed and winnowed, and the grain stored in granaries. Grapes were pressed into wine. Fruits, such as dates and figs, were dried in the sun, and their seeds were pressed to make oil.

The Egyptians grew a variety of crops. Their vegetables included lettuces, cucumbers and spring onions, cabbages, leeks and onions, along with pulses, such as peas, beans and lentils. Herbs, such as mint, thyme and oregano, were also grown to add flavour to food, along with spices such as sesame, cumin, coriander and aniseed.

But not all the crops were for food. Flax was grown for its fibres, which were spun and woven into linen cloth, or used to make ropes and mats. Papyrus reeds were cultivated for their stems, the pith from which was used to make papyrus sheets for writing on. Date palms provided wood and leaves for basket-making, as well as fruit.

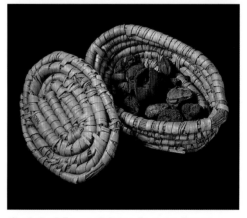

Basket of figs and dates from an Egyptian tomb. The basket was woven from palm leaves.

ANCIENT EGYPT'S RESOURCES

Ancient Egypt's enormous natural wealth was one of the reasons it became such a great civilization. The Nile gave the Egyptians fish to catch and birds and animals to hunt. The fertile earth along its banks allowed them to grow crops, make pots and build houses. Even the land that was not rich enough to farm was useful for grazing the herds of cattle, sheep and goats which Egyptian farmers kept for their meat, milk and skins.

Sandstone wall carving of a king.

Besides the farmland and pasture along the Nile, there was rock for building and sculpting. The main building rocks were limestone, found in the north of the Nile Valley, and sandstone, found in the south. Siltstone and basalt were used for sculpture.

Granite sculpture of a lion.

Calcite jar.

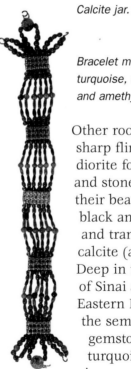

Bracelet made from gold, turquoise, carnelian, jasper and amethyst.

Other rocks included sharp flints and hard diorite for making tools, and stones valued for their beauty, such as black and red granite, and translucent white calcite (alabaster). Deep in the mountains of Sinai and the Eastern Desert were the semiprecious gemstones such as turquoise, carnelian, jasper, amethyst and emerald. From these gemstones, Egyptian craftsmen made the spectacular royal jewellery of kings like Tutankhamun.

There were other important minerals, too. Greyish-black galena (lead ore), green malachite (copper ore), and the iron-rich red and yellow earth called ochre were used as pigments in paint and cosmetics. There was gypsum for making plaster and clay for pottery.

A bag of natron.

One very important mineral was natron, which consisted largely of sodium carbonate and sodium bicarbonate. Natron had several uses. It was a detergent used instead of soap for bathing and for washing clothes – and as toothpaste. It was used to make glass and glazes. Above all, it was used to dry out bodies during mummification.

Glass amulets made from sand, natron and mineral colours.

And there were the ores of copper, tin and lead. Early Egyptian metalworkers had discovered that they could extract metal from an ore by crushing the ore and heating it in a fire until the metal separated and ran out in a molten state. This process is called *smelting*. One of the first metals they learned to smelt

Copper ore.

Tin ore.

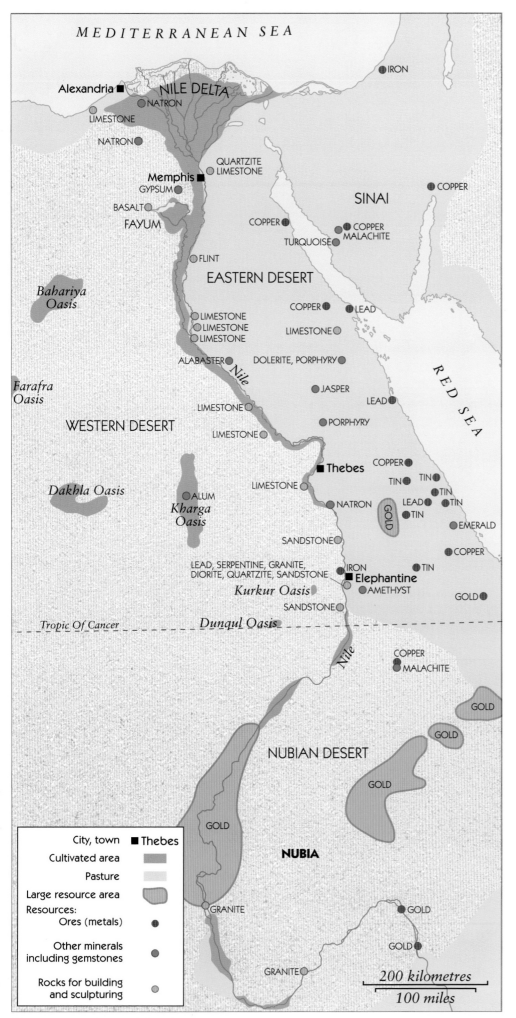

The resources of ancient Egypt.

was copper, which was quite useful, but rather soft. However, they learned that adding a little tin to the copper produced bronze, which is a much harder and stronger metal, good for making tools and weapons.

Bronze vase.

It was gold, though, that held the key to ancient Egypt's wealth. A king of Babylon once said that in Egypt gold was as common as dust. This was not quite true, but its goldmines were extremely rich. This plentiful supply of gold meant that the Egyptians could afford to import anything they needed. It also meant that they could buy the support of neighbouring countries by giving presents of gold to their rulers. This helped to ensure that those countries would be friendly to Egypt and help the Egyptians against their enemies.

Gold nugget.

Gilded wooden coffin.

TRADE AND TRAVEL

Perhaps Egypt's most important resource of all was its location. Because of the Nile, Egypt formed a natural route between Africa and the Mediterranean Sea. Via the Sinai Peninsula, Egypt was also connected to the lands lying to the north and east. Because of this, Egypt became the main trading route between Africa, Asia and Europe. This trade was the basis of Egypt's great wealth and power in the ancient world.

As early as 5,000 BC, the first Egyptians were trading tools, weapons, hunting equipment and ornaments with their neighbours – Syria and Palestine to the north, Mesopotamia (modern Iraq) to the east, and Nubia (modern Sudan) to the south. Important ideas, such as the use of writing, may have come to Egypt through trade with ancient Mesopotamia.

By the Old Kingdom (2686-2181 BC), the Egyptian government was organizing large-scale trading expeditions to distant lands. These missions were carried out by the army, together with traders. They were often away for several years. When the traders arrived at a destination, they did not always know whether the people they met there would be friendly or even speak the same language. Sometimes, the trading had to be done by representatives of each side acting out what they wanted!

As well as exporting their own products, such as grain, linen and papyrus, the Egyptians controlled the trade in exotic African goods, such as gold, incense, ebony and ivory, ostrich eggs and feathers, exotic animals and their furs. These were exchanged for silver from Syria, copper from Cyprus, olive oil

Below: Nubian traders carrying gold rings, ebony, incense and animal skins.

from Crete, cedarwood from Lebanon and lapis lazuli, a beautiful blue stone, from far-off Afghanistan.

The Egyptian traders often travelled by boat. On journeys to the north, the Egyptian boats stayed close to the Mediterranean shore. On journeys to the south, they either had to sail along the Red Sea coast or up the Nile. The problem with the Nile route was that every time a boat reached one of the Nile cataracts, the crew had to get out and drag their craft over the rocks.

Asian traders bringing horses and silver vessels to Egypt.

Ebony box inlaid with coloured ivory.

Overland routes through the deserts also played an important part in Egypt's trading network. Trading caravans travelled south to Nubia, west to the desert oases and Libya, east to Sinai and the Red Sea, and north to Syria and Palestine.

A tomb model of a boat.

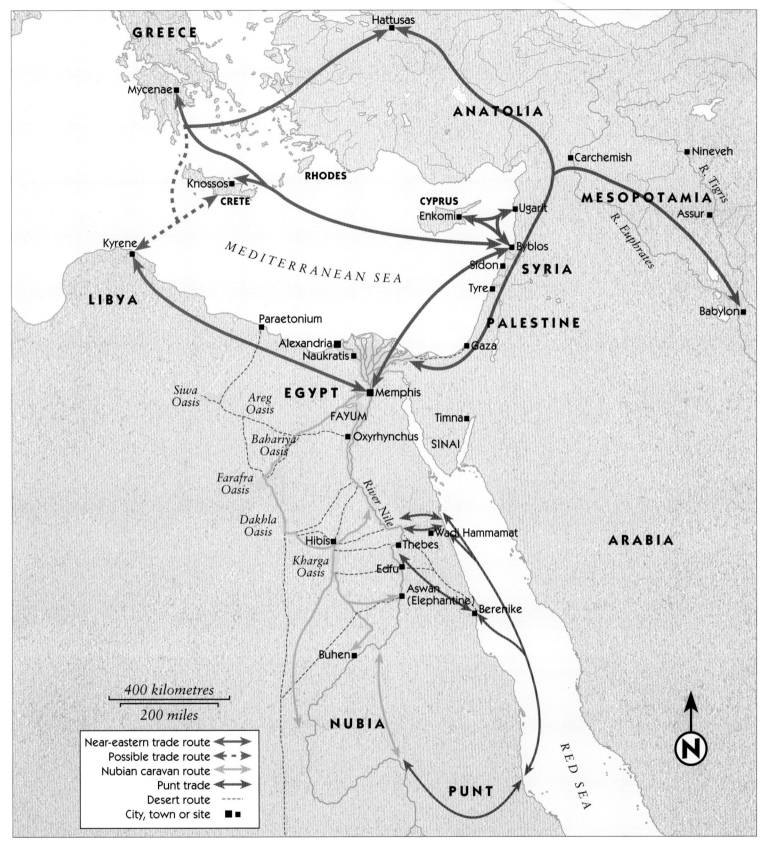

Egypt's main trading routes.

The goods were loaded on donkeys or carried on the backs of porters.

Foreign traders from Syria, Palestine and the Mediterranean also travelled to Egypt. By the 6th century BC, Greek merchants were visiting Egypt so often that they were given their own town at Naukratis in the Nile Delta. During the Persian period, a canal linking the Nile with the Red Sea was completed, making it easier to trade with Arabia, the source of incense and spices, and perhaps even with distant India.

Under the Ptolemies and the Romans (332 BC to AD 395), Alexandria was Egypt's main seaport, connecting the Nile with the Mediterranean, though Aswan kept its importance as the main market for African produce. Egypt remained an important centre of trade into the 19th century AD, when the Suez Canal was built to create a direct route between the Red Sea and the Mediterranean.

THE EGYPTIAN EMPIRE

Above: Nubians bringing tribute to Rameses II after the battle of Beit el Wali.

The Nile provided everything the Egyptians needed for their daily lives, but it was trade that made Egypt rich and powerful.

One of Egypt's priorities was to keep their control over the gold mines of Nubia, Egypt's southern neighbour. Egypt had its own gold mines, but there was far more gold in the deserts of Nubia. The Nubians were fierce warriors, but they were not as powerful as the Egyptians who occupied their lands and held them by force. The Egyptian king Senusret III (1874-1855 BC) boasted that he took control of Nubia by killing the Nubian people, stealing their animals, burning their crops and poisoning their drinking water. He built a chain of forts in Nubia to make sure that Egypt maintained its control of the region. These forts also acted as bases for Egyptian traders, miners and prospectors.

Gold from Nubia was sometimes exported to the countries to Egypt's north-east – now Israel, Palestine, Jordan, Lebanon and Syria. This region was divided into many small city-states rather than a few large countries. In one way, this was very good for Egypt, because it meant that none of the states was strong enough to threaten Egyptian territory. But in another way it was

bad, because the constant fighting between rival city-states disrupted Egypt's trading activities.

The Egyptians wanted to control these territories, too, but they did it in a different way. Instead of making this region part of Egypt, they gave the rulers of city-states gold and the protection of the Egyptian army provided that they did what the Egyptian king wanted. This had two advantages for Egypt. The region was made safe for Egyptian traders, and its territories provided a zone of protection between Egypt and its powerful enemies, such as the Hittites and Assyrians.

On the whole, this strategy worked well. At the height of Egypt's power during the New Kingdom (about

Above: Reconstruction of an Egyptian fort at Buhen in Nubia.

Right: Tile from a royal palace showing a Libyan captive.

1270 BC), the Egyptian empire stretched from the borders of modern Turkey in the north to the fourth Nile cataract in modern Sudan. However, it was a constant struggle for Egypt to

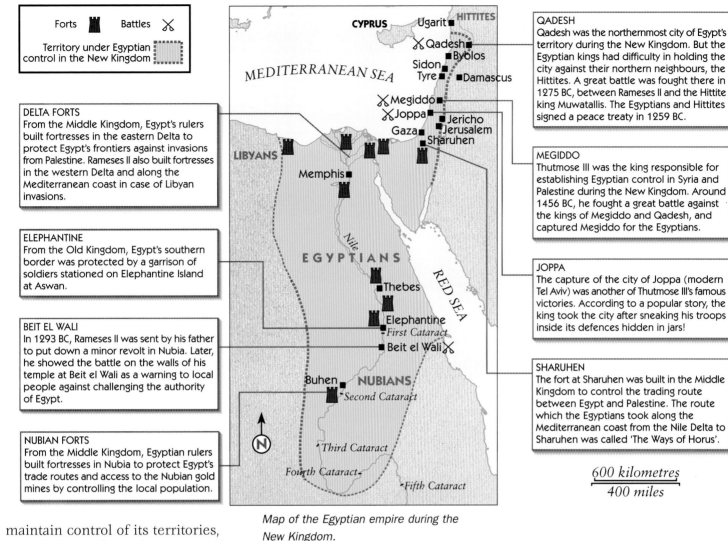

Forts 🏰   **Battles** ✕

Territory under Egyptian control in the New Kingdom ⌐⌐⌐

DELTA FORTS
From the Middle Kingdom, Egypt's rulers built fortresses in the eastern Delta to protect Egypt's frontiers against invasions from Palestine. Rameses II also built fortresses in the western Delta and along the Mediterranean coast in case of Libyan invasions.

ELEPHANTINE
From the Old Kingdom, Egypt's southern border was protected by a garrison of soldiers stationed on Elephantine Island at Aswan.

BEIT EL WALI
In 1293 BC, Rameses II was sent by his father to put down a minor revolt in Nubia. Later, he showed the battle on the walls of his temple at Beit el Wali as a warning to local people against challenging the authority of Egypt.

NUBIAN FORTS
From the Middle Kingdom, Egyptian rulers built fortresses in Nubia to protect Egypt's trade routes and access to the Nubian gold mines by controlling the local population.

QADESH
Qadesh was the northernmost city of Egypt's territory during the New Kingdom. But the Egyptian kings had difficulty in holding the city against their northern neighbours, the Hittites. A great battle was fought there in 1275 BC, between Rameses II and the Hittite king Muwatallis. The Egyptians and Hittites signed a peace treaty in 1259 BC.

MEGIDDO
Thutmose III was the king responsible for establishing Egyptian control in Syria and Palestine during the New Kingdom. Around 1456 BC, he fought a great battle against the kings of Megiddo and Qadesh, and captured Megiddo for the Egyptians.

JOPPA
The capture of the city of Joppa (modern Tel Aviv) was another of Thutmose III's famous victories. According to a popular story, the king took the city after sneaking his troops inside its defences hidden in jars!

SHARUHEN
The fort at Sharuhen was built in the Middle Kingdom to control the trading route between Egypt and Palestine. The route which the Egyptians took along the Mediterranean coast from the Nile Delta to Sharuhen was called 'The Ways of Horus'.

600 kilometres
400 miles

Map of the Egyptian empire during the New Kingdom.

maintain control of its territories, and land was always being gained and lost. Sometimes, especially when Egypt's government was weak, foreign enemies even invaded Egypt.

In the Second Intermediate Period (1650 to 1550 BC), a people from somewhere in the Middle East (probably around modern Palestine) occupied northern Egypt. The Egyptians just called them 'foreign rulers'. Usually, they are described by the Greek version of this name, *Hyksos*. At first, the Hyksos were peaceful settlers, but they gradually took control of more and more land. Then they formed an alliance with the Nubians, which left Egypt's rulers in a very dangerous position. Eventually, the Hyksos were defeated and expelled by the first pharaohs of the New Kingdom.

After this, Egypt's kings took great care to maintain control of their empire. On many occasions, they had to fight battles to defend their territories. One of the most famous battles in Egyptian history was the Battle of Qadesh, a city in Syria. It was fought in 1275 BC between Rameses II of Egypt and the Hittite king Muwatallis. Nobody won, but in 1259 BC Rameses II made a treaty with the Hittites which brought a long peace between the two nations.

A temple relief showing Rameses II at the Battle of Qadesh.

CONQUERORS AND CHANGES

Assyrians attacking an Egyptian town.

During the New Kingdom (1550-1069 BC), Egypt was the most powerful nation in the Mediterranean and Middle Eastern world, but this situation could not last forever. Although Egypt remained at peace with the Hittites after the treaty of 1259 BC, there were other, bigger, empires gaining power. Egypt's great natural wealth made it very attractive to invaders.

In fact, the next invaders to threaten Egypt were not soldiers of a great empire, but large groups of economic migrants from Libya and the eastern Mediterranean. These *Sea Peoples* had been displaced by war in their own countries, and desperately needed land to grow food and feed their animals. They were not soldiers, but a vast horde of men, women, children and herds. They first attempted to settle in Egypt around 1200 BC, but instead of welcoming and helping them, the Egyptians felt threatened and fought them off. However, they kept returning and it was almost 150 years before the Egyptians finally managed to defeat them.

The Nubian pharaoh Taharqo, protected by Amun in the form of a ram.

But fighting off the Libyans, (who were attempting to settle in the Delta,) and the Sea Peoples left Egypt weak and poor. By the end of the 11th century BC, the government had collapsed, and before long a family of Libyan kings was ruling Egypt. The Egyptians resented being ruled by foreigners, and the fighting that resulted left the country even weaker. In the 8th century BC Egypt was conquered again, this time by a Nubian ruler called Piy. Piy was the first Nubian to conquer Egypt, establishing the 25th Dynasty of Nubian kings (747 to 656 BC). They were good rulers, but while they were helping Egypt to recover, another power – the Assyrians – were expanding their territory towards Egypt's borders.

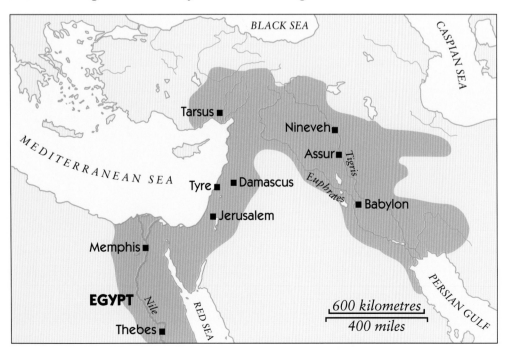

The Assyrian empire.

The Assyrians were a warlike people from the city of Assur, in Mesopotamia (modern Iraq). They first invaded Egypt in 671 BC and then in 669 BC. They occupied Egypt again in 664 BC and placed a ruler of their choice, Psamtek I, on the throne. The Egyptians disliked being ruled by the Assyrians, but at least their government was stable. This meant that the situation inside Egypt did not change too much and the country could begin to recover.

Meanwhile, the Assyrians were busy defending themselves against the rising Persian empire. Eventually, the Persians defeated the Assyrians and took control of Egypt in 525 BC. They found it difficult to control the Egyptian people. The Egyptians resisted their Persian conquerors and, for a short time, they were able to keep the Persians out and govern themselves.

But in 343 BC the Persians returned, and stayed for 11 years.

Since 336 BC, the Persians had been at war with an alliance of Greek states under the leadership of Alexander the Great. Before the second Persian invasion of Egypt, the Egyptians had supported the Greeks with supplies and troops, and the Greeks in return had helped the Egyptians resist the Persians. In 332 BC, the Greek army, led by Alexander the Great, landed in Egypt and expelled the Persians.

Unlike the Persians, the Greeks respected Egyptian traditions. For example, the first thing Alexander did on his arrival in Egypt was to make offerings to the Egyptian gods. He was crowned king of Egypt and started work on a new capital city called Alexandria, on the Mediterranean coast. After Alexander died in 323 BC, Egypt was ruled first by his half-brother and then by his son, Alexander IV. They were followed by the descendants of his general, Ptolemy.

Above: The Persian king Darius (on the right), shown as an Egyptian pharaoh.

Left: The Persian Empire.

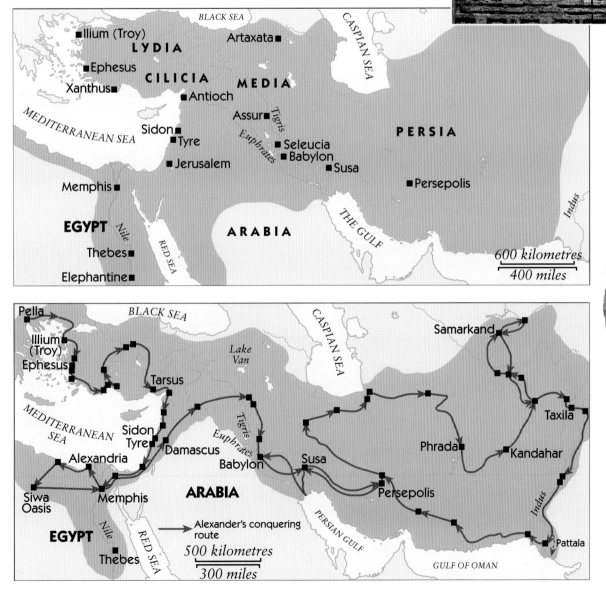

Bust of Alexander the Great.

The conquests of Alexander the Great.

AFTER THE PHARAOHS

While the Ptolemies were ruling Egypt (305 to 30 BC), a new powerful empire was growing in the Mediterranean – Rome. At first, the Ptolemies managed to stay on friendly terms with the Romans, but they were slowly drawn into Roman politics and became dependent on Rome for financial support and military protection. In an attempt to reclaim Egypt's power, the last Ptolemaic ruler, Cleopatra, persuaded her husband, the Roman general Mark Antony, to oppose Roman interference. In 32 BC, Rome declared war on Cleopatra. The following year, Octavian, the future Emperor Augustus, defeated Antony at the naval battle of Actium and invaded Egypt, which became a part of the Roman empire.

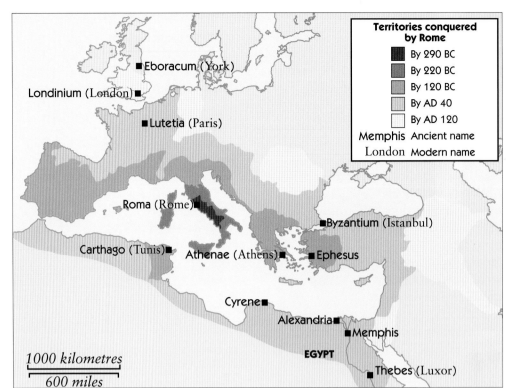

The Roman empire.

A coin showing Cleopatra.

This medieval ivory box shows the Egyptian saint Menas, who was thrown to the lions by the Romans.

A bronze head of Augustus.

Although the Roman emperors had themselves portrayed as Egyptian pharaohs, very few of them ever visited Egypt. Their main interest in Egypt was as a supplier of food to the growing Roman empire. The Romans changed the way that Egypt was governed and were harsh in their treatment of the Egyptians. There were various revolts against Roman rule, and soldiers were stationed throughout the country to keep the population under control.

In the first century AD, the new religion of Christianity began gaining converts in Egypt. At first, the Roman rulers tolerated the Christians, but as their numbers grew they became more of a threat.

Christianity had become a symbol of opposition to the Romans and a focus for Egyptian nationalism. The Romans made a new law which stated that everyone had to worship the emperor publicly. Christians who refused to do this were persecuted, and many were tortured and executed. But even this did not halt the spread of the new faith, and eventually Christianity was tolerated throughout the empire. In AD 384, the emperor Theodosius made Christianity the official religion, and the temples of the Egyptian gods were closed. Many of these buildings were reused as churches or monasteries.

In AD 395, the Roman empire was divided into the western empire, governed from Rome, and the eastern Empire, governed from Byzantium (now called Istanbul). Egypt was a part of the eastern, or Byzantine, empire, but the Egyptians were not always content. There were arguments between the Egyptians and their rulers about taxation, which was even heavier than before, and religion. Eventually, the Egyptian church, called the Coptic church, broke away from orthodox Christianity.

However, it was not long before this situation changed. In AD 641, an Arabian army arrived in Egypt, led by Amr ibn el-'As, the general of the Caliph Omar. At first, the Arabs were only interested in what they could take from Egypt, but when they saw its great natural wealth, they decided to stay. The Egyptians preferred the rule of the Muslim Arabs, who treated them better than the Byzantine emperors had. A new capital city, Cairo, was built, and in time Egypt became the centre of a great Islamic state, as famous for its wealth and learning as it had been in ancient times.

A medieval Coptic monastery.

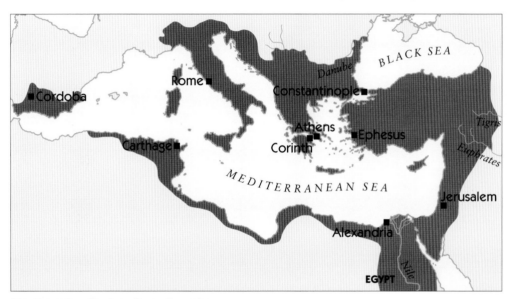

The Byzantine (Eastern Roman) empire.

A medieval mosque in Cairo.

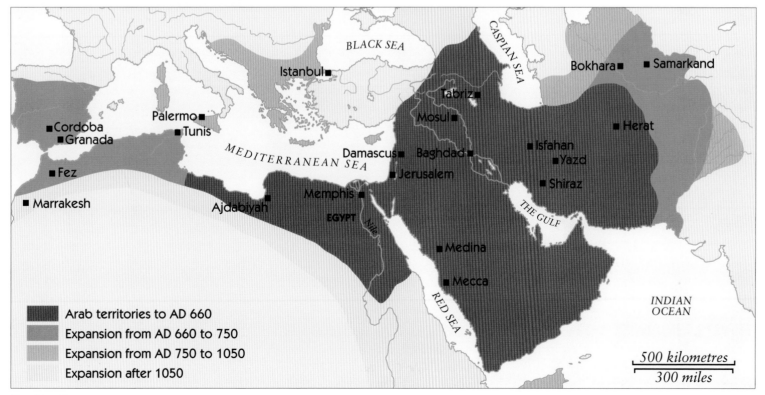

Arab territories to AD 660
Expansion from AD 660 to 750
Expansion from AD 750 to 1050
Expansion after 1050

500 kilometres
300 miles

The Islamic empire.

PART THREE
PLACES, CUSTOMS
AND BELIEFS

THE
NILE
DELTA

The northernmost part of Egypt, the Nile Delta, is also called Lower Egypt. It was formed as the Nile slowed down on the last part of its journey to the Mediterranean Sea. As the river slowed, its waters spread across the land, fanning out into separate branches. Over millions of years, the silt it deposited created a triangle of fertile land covering 15,000 square kilometres (5,800 square miles). In ancient times, there were seven main branches of the river in the Nile Delta, but now there are just two. The others have silted up.

Because the Nile's waters flow more slowly in the Delta, they spread across the land and soak deep into it, creating a moist, marshy environment that is home to a wide variety of birds and animals. In ancient times, the Delta was a favourite place for hunting and fishing. Its fertile lands were ideal for crops, such as papyrus and flax. Its lush pasture lands were far richer than those of the Nile Valley, and temples in the south sometimes sent their cattle to the Delta for fattening.

The Delta was where the Egyptians came into contact with the Libyans in the west, and the peoples of Palestine and Syria to the east. These contacts were useful for trading, but they made the Delta vulnerable to invasion. During the Second Intermediate Period, around 1600 BC, a Middle Eastern people known as the Hyksos (see page 27) occupied the Delta and established

An ancient Egyptian nobleman hunting in the marshes.

The site of Naukratis in the Nile Delta.

a capital in the city of Avaris. They were eventually chased out of Egypt, after which the Egyptian rulers took greater care to protect their borders by building fortresses.

The Nile Delta also connected Egypt to the Mediterranean world. Trading boats sailed along its branches, carrying goods to and from the capital and main port, Memphis. In

the 4th century BC, Alexander the Great founded a new capital, Alexandria, on the Mediterranean coast (see page 36). Alexandria replaced Memphis as Egypt's main port, and remained the capital until the 7th century AD.

Lower Egypt was important in Egyptian belief as one of the Two Lands. In royal art, it was represented by the papyrus plant.

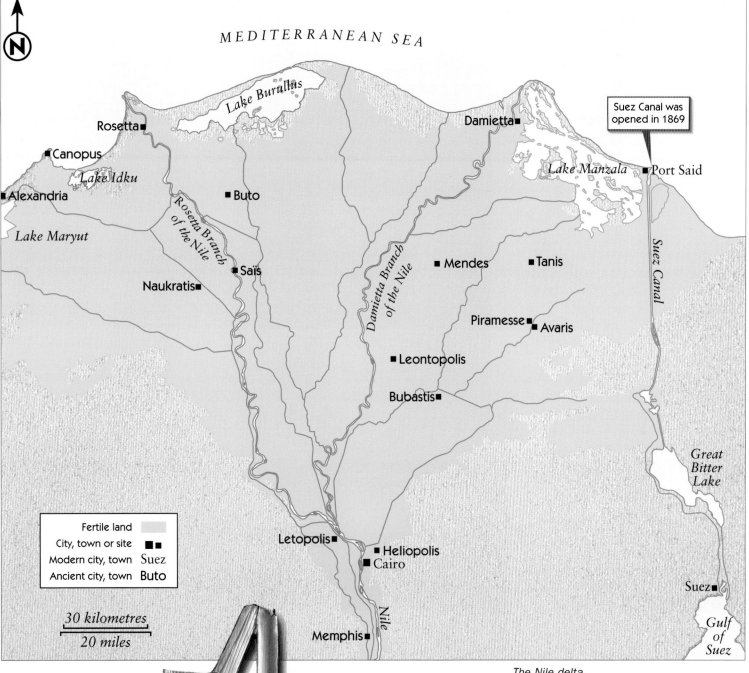

MEDITERRANEAN SEA

Suez Canal was opened in 1869

Lake Burallus

Rosetta

Canopus

Lake Idku

Alexandria

Lake Maryut

Rosetta Branch of the Nile

Buto

Sais

Naukratis

Damietta

Lake Manzala

Port Said

Damietta Branch of the Nile

Mendes

Tanis

Suez Canal

Piramesse

Avaris

Leontopolis

Bubastis

Great Bitter Lake

Letopolis

Heliopolis

Cairo

Nile

Memphis

Suez

Gulf of Suez

Legend:
- Fertile land
- City, town or site ■ ■
- Modern city, town Suez
- Ancient city, town **Buto**

30 kilometres
20 miles

The Nile delta.

The Red Crown was a part of the king's regalia, worn to signify his rule over Lower Egypt. The crown was guarded by Wadjet, the goddess of the Delta, who was often shown as a cobra.

Many of Egypt's most important cities were located in the Nile Delta, but far less is known about them than the cities of the Nile Valley. There are two main reasons for this. One is that the

Delta environment is much wetter. This means that archaeological remains are not so well preserved there, because of water damage. It is also much harder for archaeologists to work in wet conditions, because many sites have to be drained before they can be excavated. The other reason is that Egyptian cities were mostly built of unbaked mud bricks. These are very rich in nitrogen, and over the centuries farmers have taken

the bricks to break up and use as fertilizer on their fields. Some cities have literally been stolen!

Wadjet wearing the Red Crown of Lower Egypt.

Papyrus was the symbolic plant of Lower Egypt.

CITIES OF THE NILE DELTA

AVARIS

Avaris, in the eastern Delta, was the capital of the Hyksos settlers, who occupied the northern part of Egypt during the Second Intermediate Period (1650 to 1550 BC). The Hyksos colony was well organized, and settlers were allocated their own plots of land. Archaeologists excavating the Hyksos royal palace at Avaris, in 1991, were surprised to discover some Minoan wall paintings in a nearby building. This suggested that people from Crete may have been a part of the community.

ALEXANDRIA

Founded by Alexander the Great in 332 BC, Alexandria was Egypt's capital for over a thousand years – first under Alexander's successors, the Ptolemies, and later under the Roman and Byzantine emperors (see page 30). Alexandria became famous as a great centre of trade and learning. It was called the Queen of the Mediterranean, and was represented in art as a beautiful woman with a ship on her head.

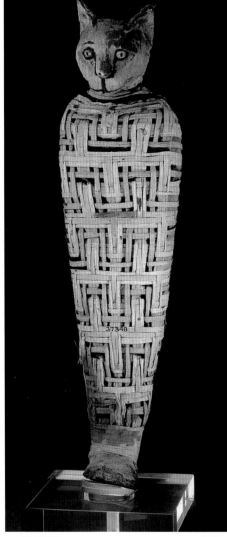

Cat mummy.

BUBASTIS

Bubastis was important as the cult centre of the cat goddess Bastet. Her temple, built of red granite and limestone, stood on an island at the centre of the city, surrounded by water. North of the city walls were cemeteries containing mummified cats sacred to the goddess.

HELIOPOLIS

Heliopolis, a Greek term meaning 'Sun City', was the centre for the worship of the sun god Ra. The temple of Ra at Heliopolis was one of the most important in all Egypt, and its priests were famous prophets and interpreters of dreams. Within the temple enclosure was a sacred stone called the Benben, which represented the primeval mound of creation from which all life had come. The Egyptians believed that the very first rays which shone from the sun had fallen upon this stone. The Benben was the model for the tall stone obelisks set up in front of temples all over Egypt, but especially at Heliopolis. Cleopatra's Needle in London and the one in New York both came from Heliopolis.

A Graeco-Roman tomb at Alexandria.

Obelisk of Senusret I at Heliopolis.

Scarab necklace from Naukratis.

NAUKRATIS

Naukratis, in the western Delta, was home to the Greek merchants who controlled the sea trade between Egypt and other Mediterranean countries. Founded in the 6th century BC, it was the first Greek town and commercial centre in Egypt. Also, it was the first and, for many centuries, the only place in Egypt where coins were struck and used as currency. It remained an important city until Alexandria was built and took over its role as a trading centre.

PIRAMESSE

The Ramesside kings of the 19th Dynasty (1295 to 1186 BC) came from the Delta. They built their chief city there, close to the Hyksos capital of Avaris, which was also the cult centre of the god Seth. Rameses II called his city Piramesse, which means something like 'Rameses' Place'. It was a heavily fortified city, protected by a moat, and besides Rameses' luxurious royal palace, there were gardens, temples, offices, housing and a military camp, where soldiers were trained for Rameses' Middle Eastern campaigns. According to the Bible, the Jews were forced to work as labourers during the building of Piramesse. It was this oppression that led to the Exodus under Moses.

SAIS

Sais was the capital of Egypt during the 26th Dynasty (664 to 525 BC), but was famous long before that as the cult centre of the war goddess Neith. Today, it is hard to imagine what the city was like, because most of its buildings were demolished and used by farmers for fertilizer. The site has never been fully excavated by archaeologists.

A figurine of Neith.

Ruins of the ancient city of Tanis.

TANIS

Tanis was Egypt's capital during most of the Third Intermediate Period (1069 to 747 BC). Its massive enclosure walls and the remains of a huge temple give the impression of a once magnificent city. In 1939, the French archaeologist Pierre Montet uncovered within the temple grounds six royal tombs belonging to kings of the 21st and 22nd Dynasties. The spectacular gold and silver coffins and jewellery he found there are now in the Egyptian Museum in Cairo.

Gold funerary mask of a king from Tanis.

SPOTLIGHT ON
ALEXANDRIA

A Roman theatre at Alexandria.

Today, Alexandria is Egypt's second-biggest city, but in ancient Egyptian times it was just a small village beside the westernmost mouth of the Nile, known as the Canopic Mouth. This changed when Alexander the Great arrived in Egypt in 332 BC. Alexander was a Greek from Macedonia, and he wanted to build a new city on the Mediterranean coast so that he could maintain contact with his homeland and the other territories he had conquered. Near the village of Rhakotis, he found a fine natural harbour, deep and sheltered, where his large fleet could anchor safely.

Here he planned to build a mighty city, unlike anything seen before in Egypt. It would be in the Greek style, with a regular grid of streets, a magnificent palace, splendid temples, shops and houses, schools, theatres and a hippodrome for chariot races. It was to be the capital of Alexander's empire, and would be named after him: Alexandria. Alexander appointed two Greek architects, Deinokrates and Sostratos, to supervise the building, but he was never to see the results of their work. The city had hardly been started when he left Egypt to fight in Persia, where he died of pneumonia just nine years later.

Alexander's body was brought back to Egypt and buried at the city's main crossroads, in a tomb called the Soma. Alexandria was protected by a wall with two main gates: the Gate of the Sun on the east, and the Gate of the Moon on the west. The main street, the Canopic Way, ran between the two. In the centre of the city, it was crossed by the Street of the Soma, which ran from Lake Mareotis in the south to the harbour in the north.

A short distance from the shore was an island called Pharos. Alexander's architects constructed a causeway that linked it with the mainland, dividing the harbour into two parts and providing it with extra shelter. The main harbour, on the east, was called the Great Harbour. The western harbour was called the Harbour of Safe Return.

Coin showing the Great Lighthouse on Pharos Island.

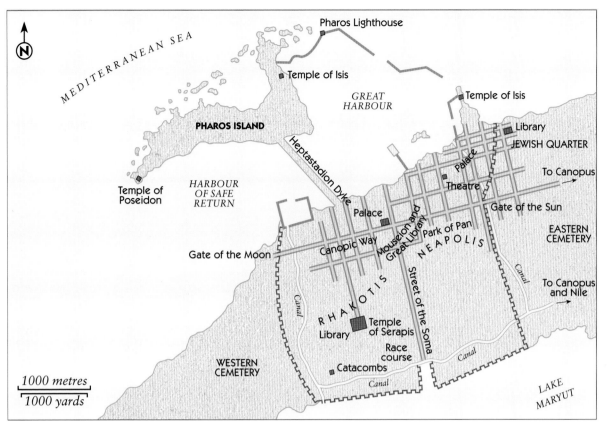

Map of ancient Alexandria.

translation of the Old Testament was written in Alexandria. It was an important centre of Christianity as well as the home of pagan philosophers. Close to the royal palace were the Great Library, housing nearly half a million scrolls, and the Mouseion, a kind of university with lecture rooms, laboratories and astronomical observatories. Among the great scientists who worked at Alexandria were the mathematician Euclid, the astronomer, mathematician and geographer Claudius Ptolemy, who produced one of the earliest maps of the world, and the astronomer and mathematician Eratosthenes. Eratosthenes not only figured out that the earth revolves around the sun, but also calculated the earth's circumference to within 400 km (250 miles) – which was not improved upon until the 18th century AD.

After Alexander died, Egypt was ruled first by his half-brother and then by his son, Alexander IV. They were followed by the descendants of his general, Ptolemy. One of these kings, Ptolemy II, had a magnificent lighthouse built on Pharos Island to guide ships safely to harbour. This lighthouse was so famous that it became known as one of the Seven Wonders of the World.

Alexandria's location made it a very cosmopolitan city, inhabited by Greeks, Egyptians and Jews, who mingled with traders from lands as far away as India. There were temples to Greek, Roman, Egyptian and Middle Eastern gods and goddesses, as well as synagogues and Christian churches. This mixture of cultures is reflected by the god of Alexandria, Serapis, who combined the qualities of the Greek gods Zeus, Helios, Hades, Asklepios and Dionysos with those of the Egyptian gods Osiris and Apis.

Alexandria was also famous throughout the ancient world as a centre of learning. The first Greek

Coin showing the temple of Isis.

The god Serapis.

Roman lighthouse near Alexandria.

THE NILE VALLEY

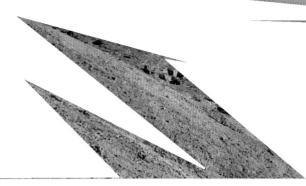

The Nile Valley, also called Upper Egypt, stretches over 700 km (435 miles) from modern Cairo in the north to the first Nile cataract at Aswan (ancient Elephantine) in the south. The Nile Valley is very different from the flat, open Delta. For most of the Valley's length, the river is hemmed in by high rock cliffs, leaving only a narrow strip of fertile land along each river bank. The climate is different, too. The further south you travel, the hotter and drier it becomes.

The Nile Valley was formed over many thousands of years by the fast-flowing waters of the river carving a course through the softest parts of the sandstone and limestone rock. Each year, the Nile floodwaters spread out as far they could, depositing silt to create a fertile flood-plain. In some places, the floodplain can be up to 70 km (40 miles) wide, in other places it is just a few metres (yards).

Above: Tomb carving showing a herdsman with cattle.

Below: Blue faience model of a hippopotamus.

Farmers in the Nile Valley grew wheat, barley, fruit and vegetables and kept goats and cows. Wild animals, such as deer and hare, were hunted in the desert, and wild birds were netted along the banks of the Nile. Fishing was dangerous because of the crocodiles and hippopotamuses in the water. An easy way to catch fish was to dig hollows to catch the Nile floodwaters and form pools. When the water went down, the fish were left in the pools, where they could easily be caught.

Many of Egypt's kings came from Upper Egypt. Early kings, such as Narmer, are shown wearing the tall White Crown which came to signify the king's rule over the Nile Valley. The White Crown was protected by Nekhbet, the goddess of Upper Egypt, who is shown as a vulture. In royal art, the south is represented by the blue lotus lily.

The vulture goddess Nekhbet wearing the White Crown of Upper Egypt.

When Egypt's first rulers were looking for a place on which to build their capital, they chose the site of Memphis, close to the junction of the Nile Valley and the Delta. This symbolized the union of the Two Lands. There were many other important cities in Upper Egypt, such as Thebes, the principal city of the New Kingdom, and Abydos, the cult centre of the god Osiris. The Nile Valley was not as vulnerable to invasion as the Delta, since it was protected on the east, west and south by mountains and deserts. Nevertheless, soldiers were stationed at the southern border to stop attacks by the Nubians.

Trade played an important part in the lives of the southern Egyptians. Dry river valleys, such as the Wadi Hammamat, connected the Nile to the Red Sea and to the Eastern Desert, and formed trading routes. The products of Sinai and the desert – such as gold, copper and turquoise – could be taken to the river along these routes, together with goods from Arabia and Mesopotamia. Aswan, on the southern border, was the main trading centre for goods from Africa, such as gold, ebony, ivory and incense. From here, they could be taken downstream by boat to cities such as Thebes and Memphis.

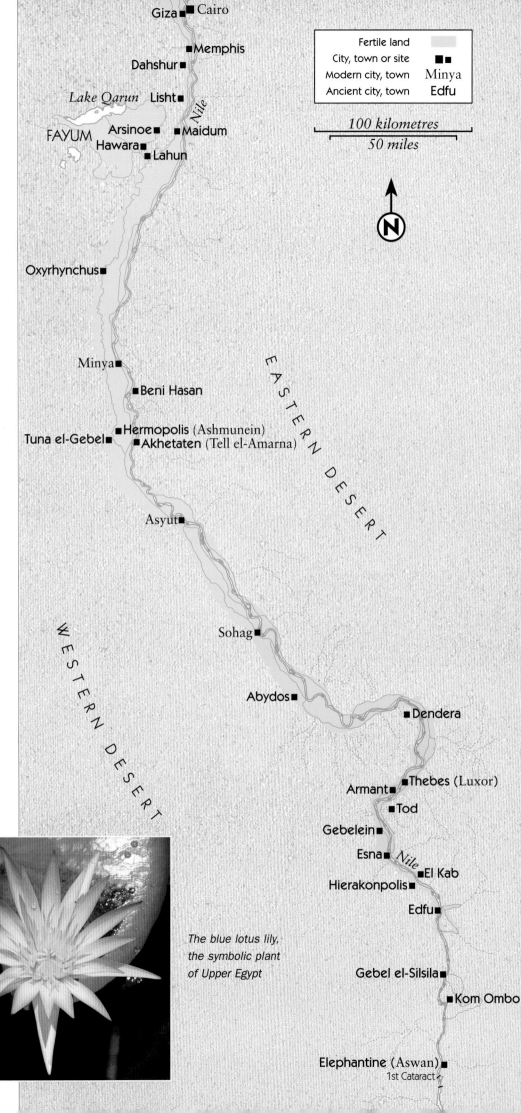

Fertile land
City, town or site ■■
Modern city, town Minya
Ancient city, town Edfu

100 kilometres
50 miles

N

Giza■ ■Cairo
■Memphis
Dahshur■
Lake Qarun Lisht■
Nile
FAYUM Arsinoe■ ■Maidum
Hawara■
■Lahun

Oxyrhynchus■

Minya■

■Beni Hasan

■Hermopolis (Ashmunein)
Tuna el-Gebel■ ■Akhetaten (Tell el-Amarna)

Asyut■

EASTERN DESERT

WESTERN DESERT

Sohag■

Abydos■

■Dendera

Armant■ ■Thebes (Luxor)
■Tod
Gebelein■
Esna■ *Nile*
■El Kab
Hierakonpolis■
Edfu■

Gebel el-Silsila■

■Kom Ombo

The blue lotus lily, the symbolic plant of Upper Egypt

Elephantine (Aswan)■
1st Cataract

CITIES OF THE NILE VALLEY

ABYDOS

Abydos was one of the oldest and most important cities of Egypt. It was the burial place of Egypt's first kings, and the chief centre of worship of the god Osiris.

The temple of Sety I at Abydos.

ARMANT

Armant was the sacred centre of Montu, the falcon-headed Theban god of war, who was worshipped at the temple there from at least the Middle Kingdom (2055-1650 BC). Montu was also worshipped in the form of a living bull, known as the Buchis bull, which was believed to be a physical manifestation of the god.

A king offering to the Buchis bull.

ASWAN

Aswan, ancient Elephantine, was built around the first Nile cataract which marked Egypt's southern border. It was an important trading centre for products brought from further south in Africa.

Aswan.

DENDERA

The temple of Dendera was the main shrine of Hathor, the goddess of love and beauty and the wife of the god Horus. Hathor was a very ancient goddess, worshipped there since prehistoric times. Many pilgrims visited the site to seek her blessing. The ancient Egyptians believed that the gods and goddesses had the power to cure illnesses, and in Greek and Roman times there was a hospital beside the temple to which the sick came to be healed.

The temple of Hathor at Dendera.

EDFU

Edfu was the sacred centre of Horus, the god of kingship. Many temples dedicated to Horus were built there from the First Dynasty onwards. The temple we can see today was built towards the end of the Ptolemaic Period. It is almost perfectly preserved, which makes it extremely interesting to Egyptologists, helping them to understand how other, more ruined, temples might have looked. Among the carvings on the temple walls is the story of Horus' battle against the evil god Seth.

Carving of Horus from his temple at Edfu.

EL-KAB

El-Kab is a very ancient city, dated to the Early Dynastic Period (3100 to 2686 BC). Its ancient name was Nekheb, and the vulture goddess Nekhbet was the local deity. The walls of the city still survive, though most of the buildings inside have disappeared. Some of the tombs at el-Kab contain interesting paintings and inscriptions which give details of life in Egypt during the New Kingdom.

ESNA

Most of the ancient remains of Esna lie buried under the modern town, but boats still tie up at its Roman quay. It is most famous for the remains of a temple dedicated to the Nile god Khnum.

Relief of the god Khnum.

HERMOPOLIS

Statue of the god Thoth as a baboon, at Hermopolis.

The ancient town of Hermopolis Magna, modern Ashmunein, got its name from the Greeks, who thought its chief god Thoth was the same as their god Hermes. Thousands of baboons and ibises, Thoth's sacred animals, were kept in his temple there, and buried nearby in underground catacombs. The ancient Egyptian name for Hermopolis was Khmunu, which means Eight-Town. It was given this name because the eight mysterious creator gods and goddesses who first brought the world into being were worshipped there.

HIERAKONPOLIS

Hierakonpolis, ancient Nekhen, lies on the west bank of the Nile, and

Early Dynastic pottery lion from Hierakonpolis.

was the twin city of el-Kab on the east bank. Its Greek name means Falcon City, because Horus was worshipped there in the form of a falcon. Hierakonpolis is especially interesting to Egyptologists because its town, temple and cemeteries continue to reveal important evidence about life and death in Egypt in Predynastic and Early Dynastic times (5500 to 2686 BC).

KOM OMBO

Carving of Sobek from Kom Ombo.

In ancient times, Kom Ombo was an important farming area and trading centre. Its unusual double temple, built by the Ptolemies, was dedicated to the crocodile god Sobek and a form of Horus.

MEMPHIS

Memphis was Egypt's first capital and the sacred centre of the creator god Ptah (see page 42). Ptah had a temple dedicated to him, where he was worshipped together with his wife, the destroyer goddess Sekhmet, and their son, the lotus god Nefertum. During the Old Kingdom (2686 to 2182 BC), Egypt's kings were buried in pyramids in the cemeteries of Memphis.

THEBES

Ancient tombs and modern houses on the west bank of the Nile at Thebes.

Thebes was the capital of Egypt during the New Kingdom (1550 to 1069 BC). Many of Egypt's most famous monuments are found there, including the royal tombs in the Valley of the Kings. The god of Thebes was Amun, who was worshipped with his wife Mut and their son Khonsu, at the temple of Karnak.

TOD

The city of Tod was south of Armant, on the east bank of the Nile. During the Middle Kingdom (2055 to 1650 BC), it was important for the temple of Montu, the Theban god of war. In 1936, the French archaeologist François Bisson de la Roque discovered an extraordinary treasure buried under the temple. Almost everything he found came from outside Egypt, and provided important information about Egypt's trading contacts during the Middle Kingdom.

The Tod treasure.

SPOTLIGHT ON
MEMPHIS

The city of Memphis lies just south of modern Cairo, close to where the Nile Valley joins the Nile Delta. Memphis was Egypt's first capital. The ancient Egyptians believed that it had been founded by Menes, the nation's first king (see page 18). All through Egyptian history Memphis was one of Egypt's most important cities, because it symbolized the union of the Two Lands of Upper and Lower Egypt. Even when the capital was somewhere else, the king always had a palace at Memphis.

Memphis is actually a Greek name. The city's Egyptian name, Mennefer, meaning 'established and beautiful', was borrowed from one of the pyramids in the nearby royal cemetery. Today, there is little left of Memphis to see. Most of the city has been destroyed, and much of what remains lies buried underneath modern villages. Fortunately, archaeologists have been able to uncover parts of the ancient city to give some idea of what it was like.

Ancient writers record that Memphis was enclosed by a city wall – one of its ancient Egyptian names was

The site of Memphis today.

The gods of Memphis: Nefertum, Sekhmet and Ptah.

White Walls. Within the walls, the most important buildings were the royal palace and the temple of Ptah, the chief god of Memphis. Ptah was a creator god, and his wife was the fierce, lioness-headed Sekhmet, the destroyer goddess who brought

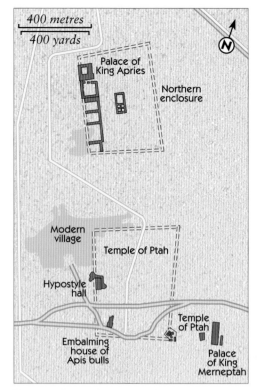

The temples and palaces of ancient Memphis.

sickness and war. Their son was the lotus god Nefertum. Until the Ptolemies built Alexandria in the 4th century BC, Memphis was Egypt's chief port. Beside the river

Reconstruction of how Memphis looked in ancient times.

Ankhwah was a shipbuilder who lived in Memphis during the Old Kingdom.

were the wharves where cargoes from distant lands were unloaded, and the shipyards where trading boats and warships were built. In offices nearby, scribes recorded the comings and goings of boats and their cargoes.

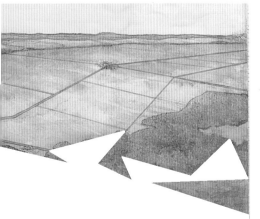

A CLOSER LOOK AT... Egyptian boats

Boats were important to the ancient Egyptians, because the Nile was the country's main route of communication. Egyptian boats were wide and shallow, with a high prow (front) and stern (back). Larger boats usually had a cabin on the deck. At the stern was a large steering oar, sometimes with a shelter to protect the helmsman from the hot sun. In the centre of the deck, a tall mast held a large, rectangular linen sail. In Egypt, the wind blows constantly north to south, so on journeys to the south, the sail was raised to help the boat move against the Nile's current. Along both sides of the boat were oars. When the boat was travelling northwards, the sail was taken down and the crew rowed the boat, helped by the Nile current.

Several different kinds of boat were in use. The smallest were the papyrus rafts, used for hunting, fishing, and ferrying people across the river. The largest were sea-going vessels, strengthened to sail in the open sea. Larger boats were made of wood. Since timber was scarce, a boat was built from many small pieces of

Model of a Nile boat.

wood held together by ropes or wooden pegs. Once a boat was in the water, the pieces of wood swelled, sealing the gaps between them and preventing the boat from leaking.

A CLOSER LOOK AT... the Apis Bull

The god Ptah was sometimes worshipped in the form of the sacred Apis bull. The Apis was a young bull chosen for its special markings, and was treated as a living form of the god. When a new Apis bull was chosen, it was crowned like a king and taken to live in a special enclosure next to the temple. Its home was like a miniature palace and had two doors, one lucky and the other unlucky. The priests claimed that they could tell the future of Egypt by seeing which door the bull used. The Apis bull was like a national mascot for the ancient Egyptians, and when one died, the whole country went into mourning.

The dead animal was mummified and given a state funeral, then buried in a huge granite sarcophagus in a special area of the cemetery at Saqqara.

SCRIBES AND WRITING

Writing first developed in Egypt in the late 4th millennium BC. Only about one in a hundred ancient Egyptians could read and write, so literacy was a highly valued skill and the entry to a successful career in government. Scribes were the civil servants responsible for the everyday running of the Egyptian state. They were involved in everything – copying out religious texts, filing diplomatic letters, collecting taxes, paying state employees, recording court cases and organizing building projects. As well as learning to read and write in Egyptian, a trainee scribe might also have to study foreign languages, mathematics, astronomy, geography or law, depending on his future post.

Scribes at work.

Statue of a scribe, writing on a papyrus roll held across his lap.

Right: Scribe's palette with reed pens and ink blocks.

A good scribe could rise to the highest posts in the land. The highest official of all was the vizier, or chief minister, who was the king's deputy and personal adviser. The vizier was in overall charge of Egypt's government, which was divided among the royal household, the army, the priesthood, the foreign service and the civil service. In practice, these departments quite often overlapped. In many towns, the royal palace and government offices were next to the temple, and soldiers and officials often had part-time jobs as priests. Inside Egypt, each town had its mayor and council, who answered to the central government.

The royal household was made up of the king's personal staff. These included a chancellor, a steward and a chamberlain, plus secretaries, wardrobe keepers, hairdressers and beauticians, cooks and all the other palace servants. The army and navy were headed by a commander-in-chief. As well as protecting Egypt's borders and fighting wars, the commander's duties included providing men for trading, prospecting and mining expeditions. The priesthood was headed by a High Priest. His job was to see that the temples were properly supplied, maintained and staffed, and that festivals and rituals were correctly carried out. Foreign affairs were managed by the governors of foreign provinces and the diplomatic service.

The first kind of writing used in Egypt was the hieroglyphic script. Hieroglyphs developed from the picture signs the early Egyptians used to write names and titles. Many hieroglyphs represented the creatures, plants and objects they saw around them.

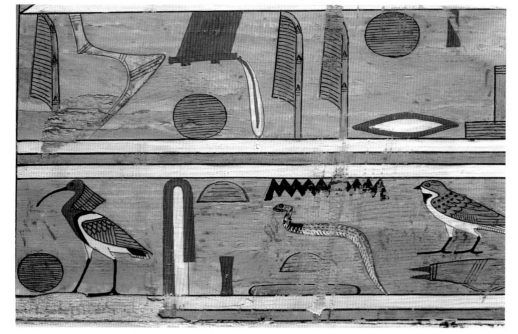

Painted hieroglyphs on a coffin.

Royal names were written in hieroglyphs inside an oval symbol of eternity, which we now call a cartouche.

Hieratic script, written on papyrus.

Hieroglyph is a Greek word which means 'sacred carving'. The Egyptians themselves called hieroglyphs the 'divine words'. The hieroglyphic script was mainly used for royal or religious texts carved in stone or wood or written on papyrus. For everyday documents, such as letters and government records, scribes used a joined-up version of the hieroglyphic script known as *hieratic*. In hieratic the complicated pictures that make up hieroglyphs were simplified to a few strokes and curves. Hieratic texts were usually written in ink with a reed brush on papyrus or on pieces of stone or pottery called *ostraca*.

By about 600 BC, a new script called *Demotic*, which means 'people's script', began to replace hieratic. Finally, around the 1st century BC, the *Coptic* script was invented. By this time, Egypt was ruled by the Ptolemies, and Greek had become the official language of the Egyptian government, though most of the population still spoke Egyptian. Coptic was developed as a way of writing the Egyptian language using the 24 letters of the Greek alphabet and six signs taken from demotic. In the 7th century AD, Arabic became the official language, but Coptic remained in use among Egyptian Christians until the 16th century and is still used in their church services.

Coptic script written on an ostracon.

Demotic script carved on the Rosetta Stone.

THE CEMETERIES OF MEMPHIS

The cemeteries of Memphis stretch along the desert plateau to the west of the city for over 30 kilometres (18 miles), from Abu Rawash in the north to Dahshur in the south. They were used for burials from the Early Dynastic Period, around 3000 BC, to the Roman Period in the first centuries AD, but they are most famous for the great royal pyramid tombs of the Old Kingdom (2686 to 2181 BC).

The first royal tombs were at Saqqara, a huge cemetery covering 30 square kilometres (12 square miles). They were not pyramids, but long, low, oblong buildings that looked like the palaces where the kings and queens had lived Archaeologists call this kind of tomb a *mastaba*, an Arabic word that means 'bench'. The first mastabas were made of mud brick, but later they were built in stone.

Stone mastaba tomb at Giza.

Reconstruction of part of the cemetery at Saqqara.

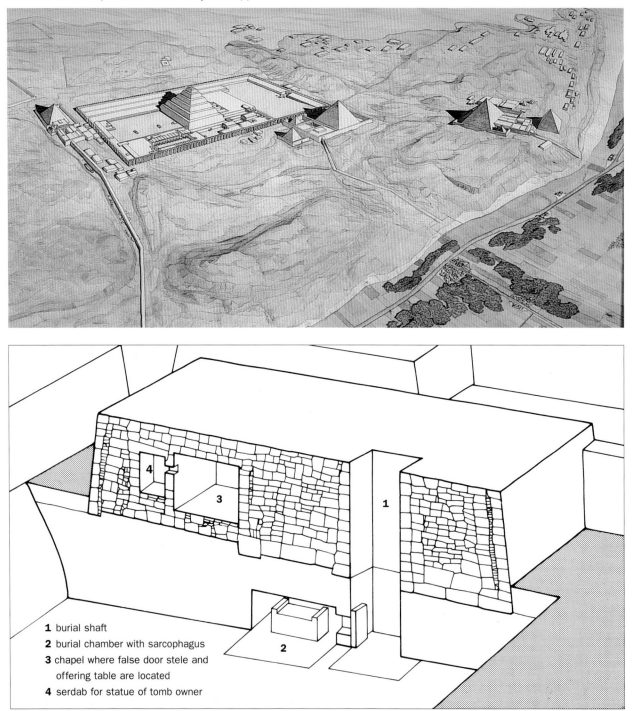

1 burial shaft
2 burial chamber with sarcophagus
3 chapel where false door stele and offering table are located
4 serdab for statue of tomb owner

Around 2650 BC, a king called Djoser decided that he wanted a special kind of tomb. His architect Imhotep built a mastaba tomb, then added a series of smaller layers on top of it to create a stepped pyramid. Nothing like it had been seen in the world before, and it made Imhotep so famous that 3,000 years later the Egyptians were still worshipping him as a god.

Around the royal tombs were smaller mastaba tombs for officials and members of the court. Inside the mastabas were chapels where

Diagram of a mastaba tomb.

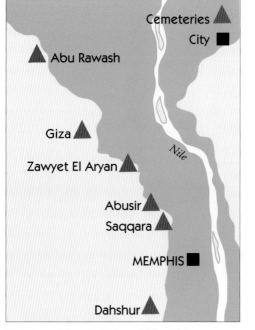

The pyramid cemeteries of Memphis.

Ibis burials at Saqqara.

Coffin for a mummified ibis.

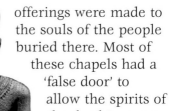
Imhotep.

offerings were made to the souls of the people buried there. Most of these chapels had a 'false door' to allow the spirits of the dead to come and go, and carvings of the things they would need for the afterlife. Sometimes, the walls of mastabas are carved with pictures of the life the tomb owners hoped to enjoy in the next world.

False door from a mastaba.

Not only people were buried in the cemeteries. At Saqqara, there were huge underground catacombs for the mummified bodies of sacred birds and animals. The Apis bulls were buried in enormous granite sarcophagi in a place called the Serapeum. There was also a separate cemetery for the cows which had given birth to the Apis bulls.

Other animals were buried at Saqqara, too. The god of the Memphis cemeteries was the falcon god Sokar, so there were falcon catacombs. There were also jackal catacombs sacred to Anubis, the jackal god of mummification.

Imhotep became associated with Thoth, whose sacred animals were the baboon and the ibis. From the Late Period onwards, pilgrims to Saqqara often offered Thoth a mummified ibis or baboon, hoping that this would earn them blessings from the god, or perhaps a cure for illness. There was such a demand for ibis mummies that there was a special breeding place nearby where the birds were raised to be killed and mummified for sale to pilgrims. Up to ten thousand ibises were buried at Saqqara every year.

The Step Pyramid of Djoser at Saqqara.

PYRAMIDS

The Giza pyramids today.

Left: Burial chamber in the pyramid of King Unas at Saqqara. The walls and ceiling are covered in sacred writing, called Pyramid Texts.

Over 80 pyramids of different shapes and sizes have been found in Egypt. Most of them were built as royal tombs during the Old Kingdom (2686 to 2182 BC) and the Middle Kingdom (2055 to 1650 BC). The very first pyramid was the Step Pyramid at Saqqara, built for King Djoser in about 2650 BC. After Djoser's time, other kings built their own pyramids in other cemeteries of Memphis, such as Dahshur and Giza. In these pyramids the steps were filled in to give each pyramid smooth, triangular sides and the burial chamber was moved from under the ground to the pyramid's interior. The Step Pyramid has a rectangular base, because it began as a mastaba tomb like the ones built for Egypt's first kings, but most later pyramids have square bases. Nobody really knows why the Egyptians chose the pyramid shape for royal tombs. Some Egyptologists think that it reminded them of the Primeval Mound in the creation myths. Others believe that it might have been meant as a staircase to allow the dead king's soul to climb up to heaven. The Pyramid Texts, magic spells carved on the walls of the burial chambers in later pyramids, often mention the king sailing among the stars in the boat of the sun god Ra.

The Step Pyramid.

Burial chambers

Burial chamber

The Great Pyramid.

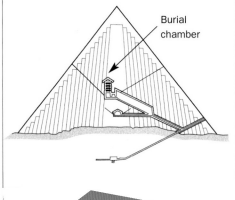

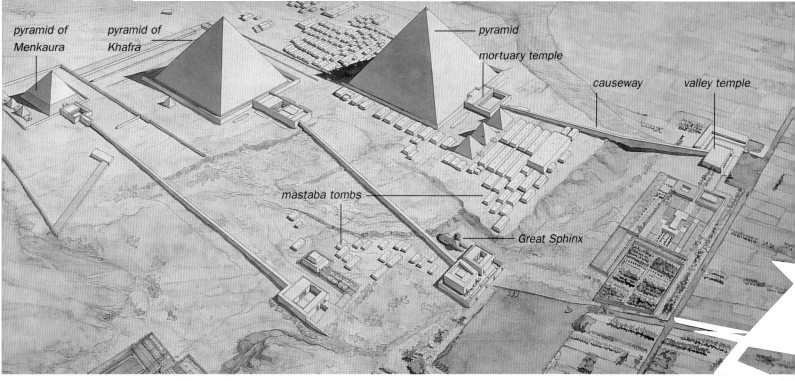

The Giza pyramids as they would have looked when first built.

The royal pyramid was just part of a whole complex of buildings meant to protect the dead king and to help him on his journey to the afterlife. Next to the pyramid was a mortuary temple, where offerings could be made to the king's spirit. The mortuary temple was joined by a covered passage or causeway to a waterside temple called the valley temple. This was where the king's body was received by the priests and prepared for burial. When the rituals were completed, the royal mummy was carried along the causeway to be laid to rest in a stone sarcophagus deep inside the pyramid. After this had been done, the passages leading to the burial chamber were sealed with heavy stone slabs. The whole pyramid complex was enclosed by a wall to keep unauthorized people out and to stop them seeing in.

The biggest and most famous pyramid is the Great Pyramid of Khufu at Giza, one of the cemeteries of Memphis. Built around 2570 BC, the Great Pyramid is almost 150 metres (490 ft) high. The sides of the pyramid were covered with smooth white limestone, polished to reflect the rays of the sun. Over two million stone blocks, each with an average

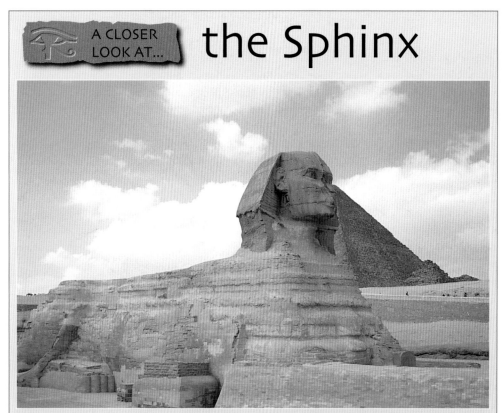

A CLOSER LOOK AT... the Sphinx

The ancient Greek word *sphinx* may come from an Egyptian phrase which meant 'living image'. In Greece, sphinxes were female, but in Egypt they were usually male. An Egyptian sphinx has the body of a lion and the head or face of some other creature, usually a human. The most famous sphinx is the Great Sphinx at Giza, which was carved from the rock left behind in a quarry which provided stone for building the pyramids. It probably represents King Khafra, and may have been made to protect his pyramid complex, because the Egyptians believed that sphinxes had magical powers to guard temples and tombs. Later, the Great Sphinx was worshipped as a form of the sun god, with its own temple.

weight of 2½ tonnes, were used to build the Great Pyramid. No-one is sure how the Egyptians were able to raise these massive blocks into place. Some experts think that the blocks may have been pushed up massive earth ramps, or lifted with levers.

SPOTLIGHT ON
LAHUN

Lahun

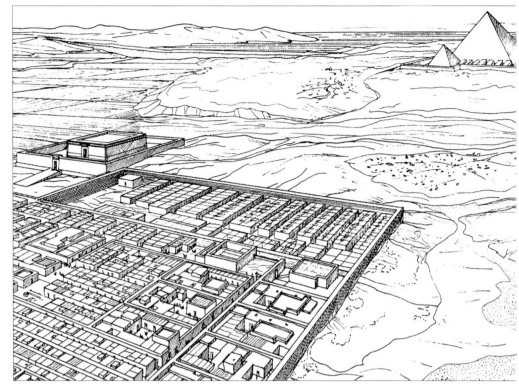
Reconstruction of Lahun.

During the Middle Kingdom (2055 to 1650 BC), Egypt was ruled by a family of kings from Thebes. They built a new capital at a place called Itjtawy (see also page 54), and were buried in cemeteries nearby. Their pyramids were built not of solid stone like those in the Memphis cemeteries, but of mud bricks, which were then faced with stone slabs.

Ancient Egyptian cemeteries were busy places. Because the king was a god, offerings had to be made to him and prayers said for him every day in his mortuary temple. The same had to be done on a smaller scale for all the people buried in the cemetery. When someone died, they left a kind of trust fund to pay for a special priest to come to their tomb and perform the proper offering rituals.

Egyptian priests were usually on duty for a month at a time, so they needed to live close to the temple where they worked. The villages where priests who worked in pyramid temples used to live are called 'pyramid towns'. One of the best preserved pyramid towns is Lahun, which was built for the priests who served in the mortuary temple of King Senusret II.

Today, Senusret's royal pyramid looks like a big pile of mud bricks, because the stone facing has been removed for use in other buildings, leaving only the brick core. Kings and queens were always buried with lots of treasures, but Senusret's burial chamber, excavated in 1887, contained only an empty red granite sarcophagus. Nearby, though, a tomb built for his daughter, Princess Sithathoriunet, contained wonderful ornaments and jewellery.

The remains of Senusret's pyramid at Lahun.

Gold headdress of Princess Sithathoriunet.

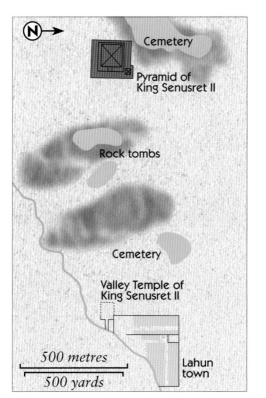

Plan of Lahun.

In ancient times, the royal tombs were protected by the priests, who checked that everything in the pyramid complex was safe and nothing was missing. One of their reports reads: 'We have examined all the goods of the temple and everything of the temple is safe and sound.'

The town of Lahun was built close to the pyramid's valley temple. It was a small walled town, covering just over a square kilometre (nearly half a square mile), and was home to around 3000 people. As well as houses, the town possessed another temple and workshops which provided the things the townspeople needed.

Archaeologists have uncovered many different kinds of evidence that tell us about the lives of the people who lived in Lahun, from letters and official records to children's toys.

A toy crocodile from Lahun.

mud bricks

The walls and buildings of Lahun were made of mud bricks, which were one of the main building materials in ancient Egypt. Mud brick is a good insulator, and so helps keep the inside of buildings cool in hot weather. That is why people living in the Egyptian countryside still prefer to build their homes from mud bricks. The ancient Egyptians used mud bricks for all kinds of buildings, from houses and offices to fortresses and pyramids. Mud bricks were easy to build with, and the raw materials from which they were made were always close at hand. The bricks were made by mixing mud with chopped-up straw and water, then pressing the mixture into wooden moulds. Mud bricks were not baked, but left in the sun to dry and to harden. Once they had dried completely, they were ready to use.

Top: Model of brickmakers.

Centre: Mud bricks drying in the sun.

Right: Modern mud brick houses.

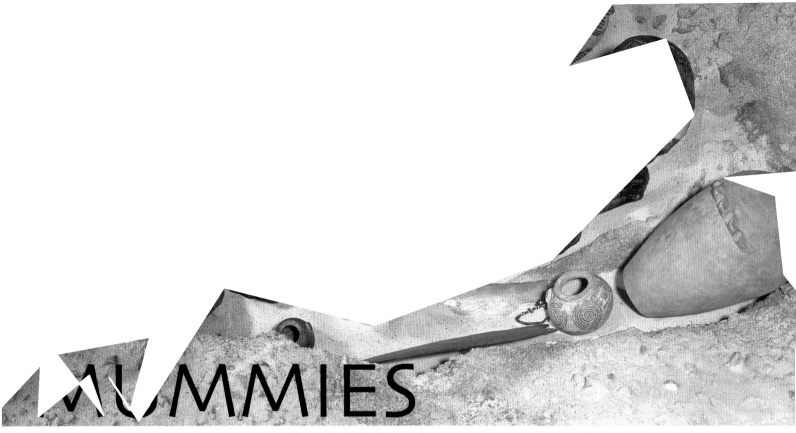

MUMMIES

The body of this Predynastic man was preserved naturally in the hot sand.

The ancient Egyptians made sure that the dead were provided with everything they were likely to need for the afterlife. They believed that people needed their bodies in order to survive after death. This meant preserving dead bodies by mummification. Only wealthy people could afford to mummify their dead. Ordinary people were simply buried in the ground. Bodies buried in the desert were sometimes preserved by accident, as the hot sand dried them out, leaving their bones, sinews, skin, hair, teeth and nails all intact. Some of these natural mummies must have been uncovered, perhaps when graves were disturbed by animals. Their lifelike appearance may have encouraged the Predynastic Egyptians to find ways to preserve the bodies of the dead deliberately. Their first attempts

Natron.

Canopic jars with the heads of the four sons of Horus who protected the organs.

were unsuccessful. Burying the bodies in wooden coffins or brick tombs stopped the sand from drying them out, and though wrapping them in bandages held the bodies together, it did not stop them from rotting.

By the Old Kingdom (about 2700 BC), Egyptian embalmers had discovered how to use a kind of salt called natron to dry and preserve dead bodies. The entire process lasted up to 70 days and took place in special tents in the desert, far away from where people lived. The

treatment which a dead person received depended on what their family could afford. In the most expensive treatment, the body was first washed, then the brain was removed. The lungs, liver, stomach and intestines were taken out through a slit cut in the left side of the body, embalmed and placed in special containers called *canopic jars*. The heart was removed and treated in the same way, but was usually returned to the body. (The Egyptians believed that the gods weighed a dead person's heart against the feather of truth to see if

*Gilded mummy
mask of a priestess.*

*Left: Mummy and its
coffin.*

Funerary amulets.

it supple, then coated in melted resin, which made it strong and waterproof. The mummy was bandaged with strips of linen, and amulets – magic charms to protect the dead person – were placed among the wrappings. There were many different types of amulet, including small figures of gods and goddesses, magic symbols or small models of things which people might need in the next life.

Finally, a funeral mask was placed over the head and shoulders of the dead person to protect them and to help the person's spirit find its way back to the body. The faces of mummy masks were often gilded or coloured gold. Gold never corrodes but stays perfect forever. The ancient Egyptians believed that the flesh of the gods was made of gold, and they hoped this magic quality would help to preserve their bodies and make them like gods, too.

The practice of mummification remained popular throughout early Egyptian history, but went into decline after Christianity became Egypt's official religion in the fourth century AD. The last known mummies date from the 6th century AD.

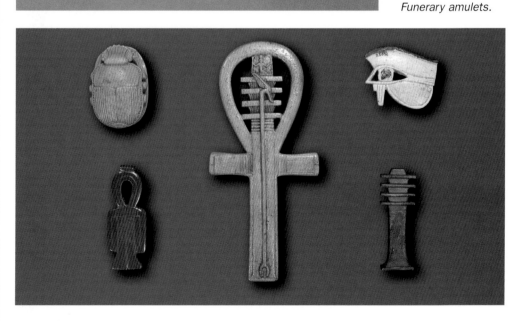

he or she deserved to go on to the afterlife.) Then the body was cleaned out and covered with the natron, which dried it out and killed the bacteria that caused decay.

After 40 days, the body was cleaned again and stuffed with linen or sawdust, together with perfumes and sweet-smelling herbs. The skin was rubbed with ointment to make

53

SPOTLIGHT ON
FAYUM

The Fayum today.

The Fayum

The Fayum is a fertile region lying to the west of the Nile and connected to it by a natural channel called the Bahr Yusef, or Joseph's River. The channel got this name because people once believed that it was built by the Bible hero Joseph during his time in Egypt. The Bahr Yusef flows into a lake now called Lake Qarun, whose shores were home to some of the first prehistoric settlers in Egypt.

The remains left behind by the people who lived in the Fayum in about 5000 BC are extremely interesting to Egyptologists. These remains show how life in Egypt changed

The ancient town of Karanis in the Fayum.

between the prehistoric Paleolithic period (Old Stone Age), when people lived a travelling life, hunting animals and collecting plants, and the Neolithic period (New Stone Age), when they settled down in villages and grew their food. Some of the Fayum people farmed for at least part of the year, but they went hunting and fishing as well. They still used stone tools, but they also built granaries in which to store their food, and learned to weave cloth and to make pots and baskets.

Later in Egyptian history, the Fayum became a prosperous farming region. When the Middle Kingdom kings moved their capital to Itjtawy, they drained some of

the marshes around the lake to create farmland, and built dams to control the water supply. They also built a temple to Sobek, the crocodile god, who was worshipped there. In the New Kingdom, the

wives and children of Rameses II (1279-1213 BC) lived in a palace in the Fayum. Some of these women supervized the textile factories that made linen for the royal court and the temples of the gods.

This parade armour, made from the skin of a crocodile, was worn to honour the god Sobek.

Writing materials from Roman Egypt. The papyrus in front comes from Hawara.

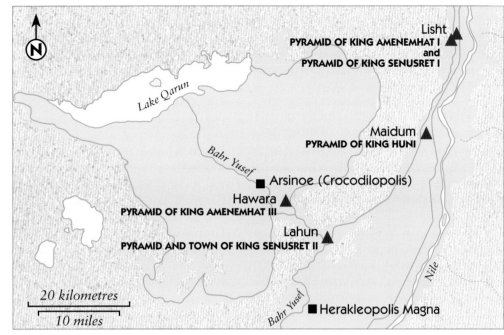

Map of the Fayum region.

These settlers spoke Greek and Latin and lived in new towns with baths and temples and apartment buildings, but they adopted many local Egyptian beliefs and customs. When they died, their bodies were mummified, but instead of wearing traditional funeral masks, their faces were covered with lifelike portraits. These so-called 'Fayum Portraits' can be found in museums around the world and are an important source of information about dress, jewellery and hairstyles in Graeco-Roman Egypt.

A Roman mummy portrait from the Fayum.

In Greek and Roman times (332 BC to AD 395), the Fayum's farmlands expanded even more, owing to government programmes for irrigation and land reclamation. New farming methods, such as crop rotation, and new kinds of plants and animals were introduced. The region also became home to large numbers of Greek and Roman settlers, many of them soldiers who had retired from the army and been given plots of land as a kind of pension.

Below: water wheel in the Fayum.

Terracotta model of a Roman soldier with an Egyptian captive.

A CLOSER LOOK AT... Fayum fossils

The Fayum is very important to geologists because the layers of rock in the desert ridges north-west of the lake reveal how this part of Egypt was shaped during the Early Tertiary Period. The oldest rocks, dating from around 35 million years ago, were formed when the Fayum was deep under the sea. They include fossils of sharks and whales. The next layer shows how the region turned to coastal marshland and contains fossils of crocodiles, giant tortoises and huge snakes up to 12 m (40 ft) long. After this, the land became forest, inhabited by monkeys and small elephants. For a while, the forest turned into a grassy plain, home to apes and other animals, but by about 24 million years ago, the trees had returned. Then disaster struck. As the continent of Africa drifted away from the Eurasian continent, the earth's crust was ripped open, and scorching lava flowed across the land, killing everything. It was not until about 70,000 years ago that winds carved out the depression that became Lake Qarun, and life in the Fayum could start again.

Arsinotherium was a rhino-like mammal that lived in the Fayum about 30 million years ago.

ANCIENT TOURISTS

From the very earliest times, the Egyptians were travelling to trade with neighbouring people. In the Fayum, finds of shells from the Mediterranean Sea show that 7000 years ago the people there were trading with their neighbours in the north of Egypt. In later times, Egyptians travelled for a variety of reasons – to attend to business, to visit relatives, or to make a pilgrimage to the temple of a god or goddess – but sometimes just for curiosity or pleasure.

In the 5th century BC, the Greek historian Herodotus recorded his travels in Egypt. Over the following centuries, it became fashionable for foreign visitors to make special trips to famous monuments such as the Giza pyramids, the Serapeum at Saqqara, the Colossi of Memnon at Thebes and the Temple of Isis at Philae. Cleopatra is said to have taken Julius Caesar for a Nile cruise on her royal barge, and in the 2nd century AD, the Roman emperor Hadrian travelled around Egypt.

Roman lamp showing pilgrims visiting an Egyptian shrine.

The Roman emperor Hadrian.

The Fayum was one of the most popular destinations for ancient tourists. Among its main attractions was the Labyrinth at Hawara, the remains of a temple attached to the Middle Kingdom pyramid of Amenemhat III (1855 to 1808 BC). This was another mud brick

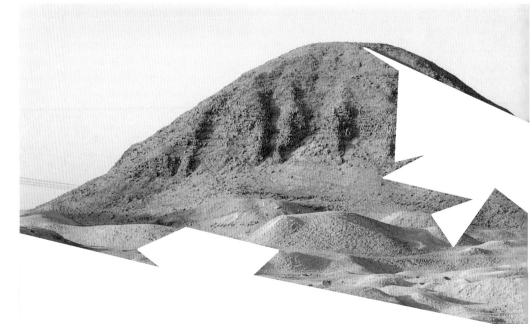

Mummified crocodiles like this one were dedicated to the god Sobek.

pyramid like the one at Lahun. The vast, maze-like ruins of its limestone mortuary temple were much admired by Herodotus, who stated that it contained 3000 rooms.

The pyramid of Amenemhat III at Hawara. The mounds at the front are all that survive of the famous Labyrinth.

Another big attraction was the sacred crocodiles. At some of the temples in the Fayum, living crocodiles were worshipped as forms of the local god Sobek. Tourists flocked to feed them, believing that if the crocodiles accepted the tourists' food they would receive blessings from Sobek. The geographer and historian Strabo, writing just before the Roman conquest of Egypt (30 BC), stated that the offerings to the sacred crocodile consisted of cakes, meat and honey, 'which are always being fed to it by the foreigners who go to see it'.

A letter from an official to the local governor of the Fayum gives details of the practical arrangements for the visit of a Roman senator to these sights:

Lucius Memnius, a Roman senator, who occupies a position of great dignity and honour, is making the voyage from Alexandria to the Arsinoite nome to see the sights. Let him be received with special magnificence, and take care that ... the customary tit-bits for Petesuchos and the crocodiles, the necessaries for the view of the Labyrinth and the offerings and sacrifices be provided.

A Nile crocodile.

The god Sobek took the form of a crocodile wearing a solar headdress.

SPOTLIGHT ON TELL EL-AMARNA

The New Kingdom pharaoh Akhenaten is one of the most remarkable figures known from ancient Egyptian history. He was the son and heir of Amenhotep III, and in 1352 BC he came to the throne under the name of Amenhotep IV. During his father's reign, the royal family had begun worshipping a sun god called the Aten as well as Amun, the god of Thebes. After he became king, Akhenaten changed his name and tried to stop the worship of Amun altogether. This brought him into conflict with the powerful priests of Amun, who had a lot of influence in Thebes. Eventually, Akhenaten and his queen, Nefertiti, gathered their family and followers together and moved the court and government away from Thebes to a new capital called Akhetaten – 'The Horizon of the Aten' – where they could worship their god in peace.

Akhetaten was unusual because nobody had lived there before. Akhenaten wanted a completely

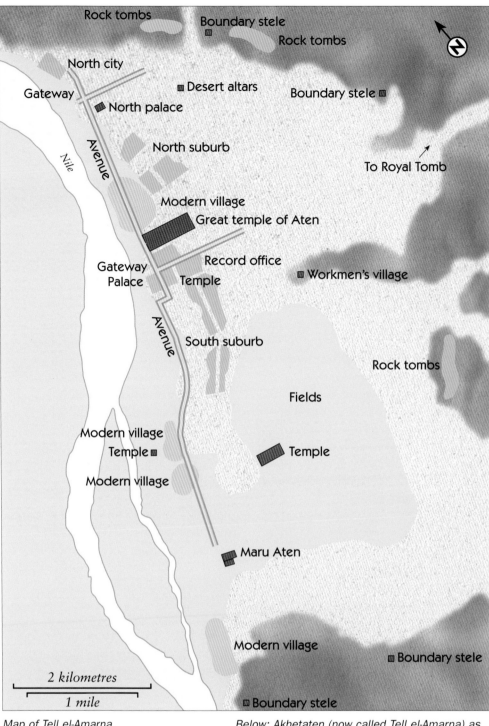

Map of Tell el-Amarna.

Below: Akhetaten (now called Tell el-Amarna) as it would have looked in Akhenaten's lifetime.

Akhenaten and Nefertiti with their daughters.

Painting from a royal palace at Tell el-Amarna.

new start, so he chose a site in the desert beside the Nile at a place now called Tell el-Amarna. The new city was founded around 1350 BC, but many of its buildings were never finished, and after Akhenaten died it was abandoned. Nothing else was built on the site until many centuries later, so parts of the ancient city are quite well preserved. The fact that Akhetaten was inhabited for only about 20 years also makes it particularly interesting to archaeologists because the evidence from the site helps to give them a picture of life there during this short period of time.

Between 20,000 and 50,000 people lived and worked in Akhetaten during the time it was occupied. The most important area was the city centre, a complex of official buildings which included royal palaces, government offices and temples dedicated to the Aten. Most people, though, lived in the city's suburbs. As well as houses, archaeologists have found stores and workshops, bakeries, wells and

even artists' studios. Artists in Akhetaten had their own distinctive style (sometimes called the 'Amarna style'), using flowing lines and vivid colours. They loved to represent

scenes from the natural world, and many of the houses and palaces of Akhetaten were decorated with paintings of plants and wildlife.

Signet ring with the name of Akhenaten.

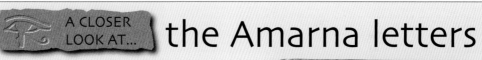

A CLOSER LOOK AT... the Amarna letters

One of the most fascinating discoveries from Akhetaten is a collection of over 300 clay tablets found in the official records office in the city centre. Most of them are letters sent to the Egyptian court from other countries and city-states in the Middle East, written in the Akkadian language.

The reason these tablets are so interesting is that they contain a great deal of information about Egypt's foreign relations during the reigns of Akhenaten and his father. Akhenaten was not very concerned about caring for the Egyptian empire, and many of the letters are from his allies pleading for support against enemies who are threatening them. One letter says: 'Let the king take care of his land, and let him send troops. For if no troops come in this year, the whole territory of my lord, the king, will perish.'

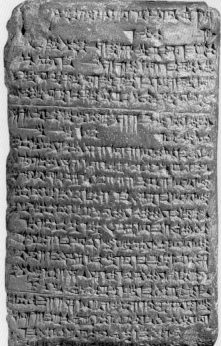

One of the Amarna letters.

SPOTLIGHT ON
ABYDOS

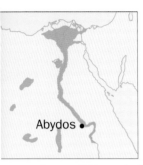

Abydos •

Abydos was inhabited from prehistoric times and may even have been Egypt's first capital. In Early Dynastic times, it was the burial place of Egypt's first kings, who were laid to rest in brick-lined pits, each marked by a stone slab, or stela, carved with the king's name. Later Egyptians thought that one of these tombs contained the body of the god Osiris, so from the Middle Kingdom (2055 to 1650 BC) onwards, Abydos became the main centre of his worship.

Osiris was the god who gave the ancient Egyptians hope of a life after death. He was the son of Geb, god of the earth, and Nut, the sky goddess. He became the first king of Egypt. The Egyptians believed that Osiris taught men how to farm the land, and that his wife Isis taught women how to spin and weave.

Plan of Abydos.

Reconstruction of ancient Abydos.

Osiris was murdered by his jealous brother, Seth, who cut his body into pieces and scattered them throughout Egypt. Isis collected these pieces together and buried them at Abydos. Even though she was the goddess of magic, Isis could not bring her husband back to life. But Osiris did rise again to become king of the dead. His son, the falcon god Horus, became king of Egypt.

The way Osiris died and was reborn reminded the ancient Egyptians of the way in which the seeds of their crops were scattered and buried, then sprouted, grew and produced

Statue of an official holding a shrine with images of Horus, Osiris and Isis.

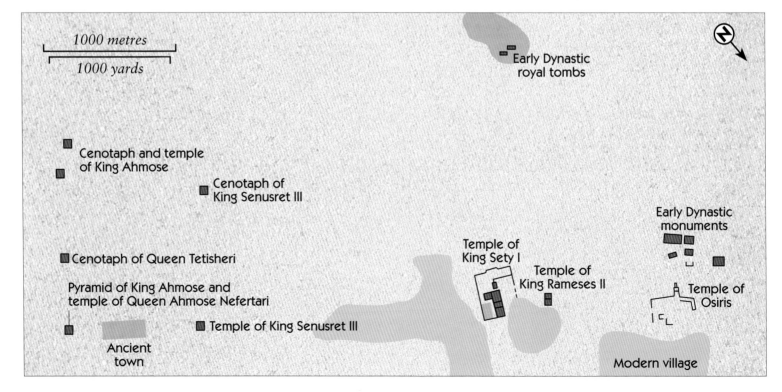

1000 metres

1000 yards

Early Dynastic royal tombs

Cenotaph and temple of King Ahmose

Cenotaph of King Senusret III

Early Dynastic monuments

Cenotaph of Queen Tetisheri

Temple of King Sety I

Temple of King Rameses II

Temple of Osiris

Pyramid of King Ahmose and temple of Queen Ahmose Nefertari

Temple of King Senusret III

Ancient town

Modern village

The ancient Egyptians believed that every king of Egypt was, during his lifetime, a living form of the god Horus, and that when he died he became one with Osiris. Many of Egypt's rulers built themselves memorial temples at Abydos, where they would be worshipped as Osiris after their death. The most famous temple was built by Sety I (1294 to 1279 BC) and includes a dummy tomb, or cenotaph, modelled on the tomb of Osiris. Every year the king presided over a great festival at Abydos, during which the death and resurrection of Osiris were acted out. It was believed that this would ensure the stability and prosperity of Egypt in the coming year.

Model boats were placed in tombs so the souls of the dead could travel to the festival of Osiris at Abydos.

seed for the next year's harvest. Osiris became the god of agriculture, and was usually shown with his skin coloured black, like the soil of Egypt, or green, like the new growth of plants. Because he was a king who died, he is represented as a mummy wearing a tall crown with horns and feathers, and holding a crook and flail, the symbols of royalty.

Because Osiris was the ruler of the underworld, people believed that being buried close to him at Abydos would guarantee them a good afterlife. The temple area is surrounded by vast cemeteries, which remained in use until Roman times. People buried elsewhere sometimes had paintings or models in their tombs showing their mummies being taken to Abydos, so that their souls could make the journey there after death. Others set up stelae or cenotaphs close to the temple at Abydos. They believed that this would allow their souls to participate in the divine rituals and festivals of Osiris.

Carving of Isis and Osiris in Sety I's temple at Abydos.

TEMPLES

Temples were the focus of ancient Egyptian religion. The Egyptians believed that as long as their gods and goddesses were content, they would look after Egypt and its people. To help to keep the deities happy, the Egyptians built them beautiful temples where their statues were worshipped.

The pylon of Edfu temple.

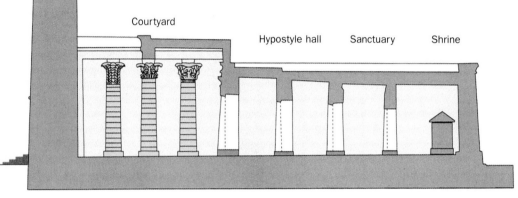

Cross section of the temple of Isis at Philae.

The ancient Egyptians believed that the statues in temple sanctuaries were the bodies of the gods and goddesses, and that the priests and priestesses were like their servants. Every day, they bathed and dressed the divine images, put make-up and perfume on them, offered them flowers and incense, and served them delicious meals. Pictures of

Hypostyle hall (hall of columns) in the Temple of Khnum at Esna.

The Egyptian term for a temple was 'God's House', and people believed that the god or goddess of the temple really lived there, in the form of a divine image kept in the temple sanctuary.

The first Egyptian temples were small shrines built to house the images of local deities. These early shrines were small buildings made from reeds or mud brick. As time passed, stone was used instead, and temple buildings became bigger and grander. The basic parts of an Egyptian temple were an enclosure wall, a courtyard, a room for offerings and a sanctuary. From the New Kingdom (1550 to 1069 BC) onwards, an important temple included massive gateways, called *pylons*, and a great *hypostyle* hall which was crowded with columns.

Statue of the god Amun.

The divine image was kept in a stone shrine, like this one from Philae.

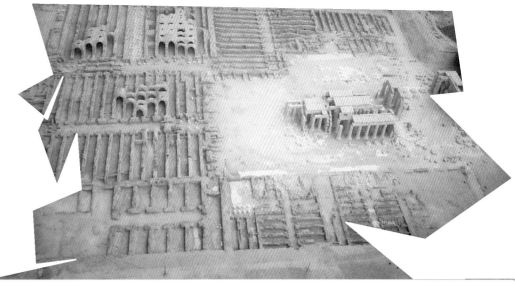

An aerial view of the Ramesseum at Thebes, showing the stores and offices where temple officials worked.

the king performing these rituals were carved on temple walls as magic substitutes for the real thing. This ensured that the gods and goddesses would always be cared for, even if nobody came to make the offerings.

The sanctuary was the holiest part of the temple, and the only people who were allowed to enter it were the king and high-ranking priests or priestesses. Egyptian temples did not have a congregation, like a synagogue, church or mosque. Only priests and priestesses were allowed inside the temple building. Ordinary people had to pray in the courtyard in front of the temple, or at

Rameses III leads a procession of priests carrying the boat shrine of the god Sokar.

special places outside the enclosure wall. Another opportunity for the population to worship their gods and goddesses was during festivals, when the divine images were carried out of the temple in procession, in shrines mounted on model boats.

Temples were not just places of worship. They were more like small, busy towns, with stores, offices, workshops, libraries, kitchens and schools for training scribes and priests. Law courts often met in temple courtyards, so that the gods would see justice done. The local government offices were often part of the temple, too. The priests were in charge of collecting taxes for the state and paying government employees. In return, they were paid with shares of the offerings given to the gods and goddesses.

Important temples were supported by the state with grants of land and goods. They owned huge estates in Egypt and abroad, as well as mines and fleets of ships, and they employed thousands of people. Most of the priests were government officials who worked in the temple on a rota of one month in four. Priests on duty in the temple had to follow many rules. They had to live apart from their wives, give up eating certain foods, shave all the hair from their heads and bodies and take two cold baths every day!

Bronze figure of a priest of Amun.

SPOTLIGHT ON
THEBES

Thebes •

Thebes, the Greek name for the ancient town of Waset, was one of the most important cities of ancient Egypt. Its modern name, Luxor, came from the first Arabs to arrive there. When they saw the remains of its great temples, they called them el-Uqsur, which means 'The Palaces'.

Thebes first became important during the Middle Kingdom (2055 to 1650 BC) and reached the height of its power during the New Kingdom (1550 to 1069 BC), when pharaohs were buried in the Valley of the Kings. By the Late Period (747 to 332 BC), the capital had returned to the north, but a powerful dynasty of Theban priestesses, the Divine Wives of Amun, had an important political role. Even in Roman times (30 BC to AD 395), Thebes was an important city and an army garrison was stationed there.

The god of Thebes was Amun, a creator god, who was worshipped with his wife Mut and their son, the moon god Khonsu. During the New Kingdom, Amun was combined with the sun god Ra to create a new god, Amun-Ra. Amun-Ra became the chief state god of Egypt, and his priests became so powerful that they were able to influence the government. King Akhenaten tried to take their power away by making the Aten the national god instead of Amun (see pages 58-59), but he was successful only for a time. After his death, the worship of Amun became more important than ever.

It was during the Middle Kingdom that Thebes began to change from a small town into a great imperial city. The 11th Dynasty king Nebhepetra Mentuhotep (2055 to 2004 BC), whose family came from Thebes, built himself a spectacular funeral monument, half-tomb and half-temple, at Deir el-Bahri on the Nile's west bank. Directly opposite, at Karnak on the east bank, he built a temple. Over the centuries, kings built new palaces. Around the temples and palaces grew up the homes of the nobility and the working people who served them.

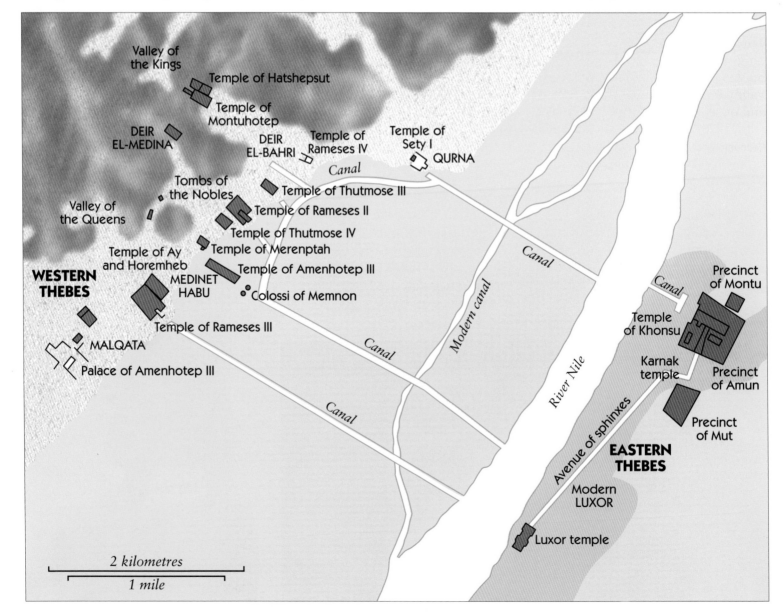

Carving of Nebhepetra Mentuhotep from his temple at Deir el-Bahri.

Rameses II with the deities of Thebes: Amun, Mut and Khonsu

The cemeteries of Thebes were scattered among the limestone cliffs on the west bank of the Nile. Because there was hardly any flat land for building, tombs were cut directly into the sides of the hills. Throughout the New Kingdom, kings and princes were buried in hidden, rock-cut tombs deep in the Valley of the Kings, while queens and other royal children were

Reconstruction of ancient Thebes.

buried in the Valley of the Queens. Clustered among the hills on the desert edge are thousands of smaller tombs belonging to ordinary people and to the nobles and officials who served Egypt's rulers.

There were many close links between the city of the living on the east bank of the Nile and the city of the dead on the west bank. One of the most important festivals of Thebes was the Beautiful Festival of

the Valley, held each spring. During the festival, the divine images of Amun and the other gods and goddesses of Thebes were taken across the river to visit the temples and cemeteries on the west bank, accompanied by the townspeople of Thebes, dressed in their best clothes and wearing garlands of flowers. In the evening, people went by torchlight to the tombs of their relatives, where they spent the night feasting.

NEW KINGDOM PHARAOHS

Some of Egypt's most famous pharaohs lived in Thebes during the New Kingdom (1550 to 1069 BC). The title Pharaoh comes from the Egyptian name for a royal court or palace – Great House. In the New Kingdom, Egyptians began to use it as a respectful way to speak of the king, in the same way that we refer to 'Number 10' when speaking of the British Prime Minister or to 'The White House' for the US President.

The New Kingdom began with Ahmose (1550 to 1525 BC), who was responsible for finally expelling the Hyksos invaders from the Nile Delta. His descendants were known as the 18th Dynasty. The first 18th Dynasty kings were very energetic. They reformed the Egyptian government, expanded Egypt's empire and developed Thebes into a great imperial city. One of the greatest empire-builders was Thutmose III (1479 to 1425 BC), who led many daring campaigns in Syria and Palestine.

By the time of Amenhotep III (1390 to 1352 BC), Egypt was extremely wealthy, and the royal family lived a life of luxury in a magnificent new palace at Malqata on the Nile's west bank. Things changed dramatically in the reign of Amenhotep's successor, Akhenaten, who tried to reform Egypt's religion and moved the capital to Tell el-Amarna (see pages 58-59). But Akhenaten's reign was short-lived, and the throne passed to his young son Tutankhamun.

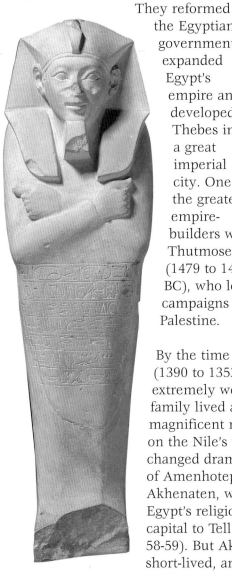

Shabti of Ahmose I.

Thutmose III.

Right: Limestone statue of Amenhotep III.

Rameses II.

Papyrus painting of Rameses III.

Tutankhamun was only nine when he became king, and he died just nine years later, with no son to follow him. The kingship passed first to his vizier (chief minister) Ay, then to his general Horemheb. Horemheb left the throne of Egypt to his general Rameses, who became Rameses I, the first ruler of the 19th Dynasty (1295 to 1186 BC). Rameses' family came from the Nile Delta and were famous warrior kings. His son Sety I and grandson Rameses II fought many battles to regain Egypt's empire. They made Egypt wealthy and powerful, and left behind many spectacular monuments.

Many of the the kings of the 20th Dynasty were also called Rameses. The most famous was Rameses III (1184 to 1153 BC), who defended Egypt against invasions by Libyans and Mediterranean invaders called the Sea Peoples. He commemorated his victories in scenes carved on the walls of his magnificent memorial temple at Medinet Habu, on the west bank of the Nile at Thebes.

A CLOSER LOOK AT... queens

Nefertari with the goddess Hathor.

Not all New Kingdom rulers were men. One of the most famous pharaohs, Hatshepsut, was a queen who ruled Egypt in her own right. Hatshepsut was the daughter of King Thutmose I and the wife of Thutmose II. When her husband died, her stepson, the crown prince, was still a child, and at first she ruled on his behalf. Later she claimed she was Egypt's rightful ruler, and was crowned 'king' in 1473 BC. Hatshepsut's reign was peaceful and prosperous. She sent trading expeditions as far north as Byblos in Lebanon and as far south as Punt in Somalia, as well as building many fine monuments to Amun.

Royal wives and mothers were often

Left: Hatshepsut dressed as a king.

very powerful, too. Nefertiti was the wife of Akhenaten and his closest supporter, appearing beside him on most of his royal monuments. Her mother-in-law, Queen Tiy, the wife of Amenhotep III, was also a powerful

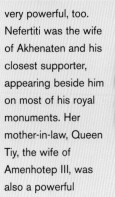

Nefertiti.

queen. After her husband died, she took over much of the diplomatic correspondence between the Egyptian government and foreign rulers, making sure that Egypt stayed at peace with its neighbours. Another famous queen, Nefertari, was the wife of King Rameses II. Rameses built her a temple at Abu Simbel in Nubia, and when she died, she was buried in a beautiful tomb which he had prepared for her in the Valley of the Queens.

IMPERIAL THEBES

The history of Thebes is reflected in its buildings, but, as in other places in Egypt, it is mainly religious buildings – tombs and temples – which have survived. The way that the temples of Thebes developed tell us a great deal about how temples were built and what they were used for. Each addition to a temple provides evidence for the king or queen who had it built, and helps to improve our understanding of Egyptian history.

The most important institution in Thebes was the great Temple of Amun at Karnak, which was begun during the Middle Kingdom (2055 to 1650 BC) and extended over the next 2,000 years. Karnak was the site of many temples – besides the temple of Amun, there were temples for his wife Mut, their son Khonsu, and Montu the Theban god of war as well as many other deities.

The Karnak temples were connected to Luxor Temple by roads lined with sphinxes. At festival times, the statues of the gods and goddesses were carried in procession along these roads, cheered on their way by crowds lining the route. Each year, during the festival of Opet, the divine images of Amun and the other gods and goddesses of Karnak were taken by river from Karnak to Luxor in magnificent barges covered with gold and jewels.

Every ruler of Egypt wanted to show respect to the gods and goddesses, and to get their divine support, by adding his or her own buildings to important temples. By Roman times, Karnak had become a rambling complex of shrines, halls, pylons, statues and obelisks covering 3 square kilometres (1¼ square miles). As well as the usual offices, workshops, schools and libraries, there were gardens with flower beds and trees, a lake and even a yard for Amun's sacred geese. The main entrance was connected to the Nile by a canal, and there was a harbour for the gods' barges and a quay where boats could tie up.

Above: The temple of Amun at Karnak.

The pylon of Luxor temple.

the latest king as the defender of Egypt, punishing foreign enemies and being rewarded by the god or goddess of the temple. At Luxor Temple, King Rameses II (1279 to 1213 BC) had his pylon carved with scenes of his great battle against the Hittites at Qadesh in Syria (see page 27).

Rameses II was not the last to add to Luxor Temple. In Roman times, soldiers stationed nearby built a chapel to their divine emperors. In Christian times, it was used as a church. Today, a mosque built over part of the temple serves Luxor's Muslim population.

Reconstruction of eastern Thebes showing Karnak (top) and Luxor Temple.

Rameses II offering to the god Amun.

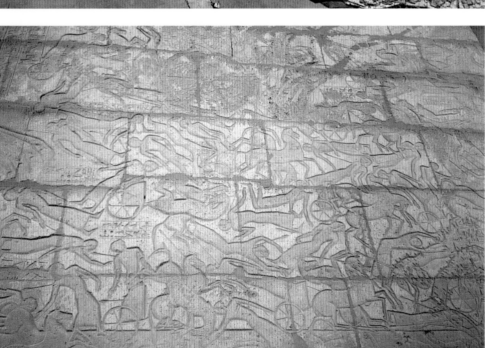

Detail of Rameses II's relief on the pylon of Luxor Temple, showing the battle of Qadesh.

Kings and queens also liked to extend temples to impress their subjects. The usual way a ruler did this was to have something with his own image added to the outside of an important temple so that everyone passing would see it. This could be a pair of statues or obelisks, but adding a pylon, or ornamental gateway, was especially popular.

A pylon provided a large space for the king to advertise himself, while conveniently hiding the monuments of earlier rulers. Painted in bright colours, a pylon could be seen by everyone in the surrounding countryside. It was usually carved with images showing

THE CEMETERIES OF THEBES

During the Old Kingdom (2686 to 2181 BC), Egypt's kings had been buried in pyramids in cemeteries built on the broad desert plateau to the west of Memphis, surrounded by the mastaba tombs of their families and courtiers. But at Thebes, where the high limestone cliffs of the Nile Valley reach almost to the river, there was no space to build pyramids or mastabas. Instead, underground tombs were cut into the cliffs on the west bank of the river.

The cemeteries of Thebes contain burials of people from all walks of life, from ancient times to the

The memorial temple of Queen Hatshepsut at Deir el-Bahri.

Left: Aerial view of the Theban west bank, showing the tombs of the nobles.

Rock-cut tombs in the Theban cemetery.

Below: Section through a rock-cut tomb, showing the offering chapel and, below, the burial chamber.

present day. The first royal tomb in the Valley of the Kings was built for King Thutmose I (1504 to 1492 BC) at the beginning of the New Kingdom. His architect, Ineni, later boasted how he had built the tomb in secret: 'nobody seeing and nobody hearing'. The tomb was hidden away in a remote valley in the desert mountains and its entrance was disguised so that once the king was buried, nobody would be able to find it.

This new type of tomb meant that offerings to the spirits of the dead kings were no longer made near their burial places. Instead, the New Kingdom pharaohs built themselves

Tomb statue of a Theban nobleman
and his wife.

A CLOSER LOOK AT... tomb paintings

In some periods, the walls of tomb chapels were decorated with brightly coloured paintings of the life the dead hoped to enjoy in the next world. The nature of the rock in the cliffs of Thebes varied from place to place, so the tomb painters could not always get a smooth surface to work on. When this happened, they had to cover the walls with a thick layer of mud plaster and then paint on top of the plaster. The colours they used still look bright because they were made from minerals, including carbon (soot) for black, gypsum (plaster of Paris) for white, ochre (iron-rich earth) for red and yellow, and malachite and azurite (stones which contained copper carbonate) for green and blue.

Painting from a tomb at Thebes.

magnificent memorial temples on the Nile's west bank, close to the edge of the flood plain. The kings could use these temples during their lives, and be worshipped there after they died. Some of these temples had small palaces attached, where kings could stay during religious festivals.

Private tombs at Thebes were not hidden, and the families of the dead would often visit them to pray and to make offerings. Most private tombs had a courtyard, an offering chapel cut into the hillside, and a burial chamber hidden below

ground. Some had a mud brick pyramid on the roof. In the courtyard, there was usually a stela inscribed with the names and titles of the tomb owner, and with prayers asking passers-by to pray for him or her. In the tomb chapels of the wealthy, there were statues of the dead. Like the tombs, these statues usually faced east. The Egyptians believed that this would help the dead to be born again with the rising sun.

Stela (stone memorial slab) of the official Tjetji. It is carved with pictures of food, drink and other offerings to make sure that Tjetji would have everything he needed for the next life.

PROVIDING FOR THE DEAD

Funeral procession and (on the right) the Opening of the Mouth ceremony.

Egyptian beliefs about the afterlife were quite complicated. Preparations for a person's burial began during their lifetime with the construction of the tomb and the assembling of the funeral goods and offerings. These included food and drink, as well as clothes, furniture and writing equipment.

Models of bakers, brewers and butchers were put in tombs so that the dead person would always have plenty to eat and drink.

Above: Loaves of bread from a tomb.

Pottery soul house with models of food offerings.

Left: Page from a Book of the Dead, showing the Fields of Reeds.

Right: Tomb model of a servant carrying food offerings.

But it was not enough to have just a tomb and offerings. The body of a dead person had to be mummified and protected with magic spells, amulets and ceremonies. Poor people who were not able to afford these expensive preparations were not mummified, but simply wrapped and buried in the ground with a few simple offerings, such as a 'soul house', a pottery model of a house containing models of the things they would need for the next life.

scarabs

One of the most important funeral amulets was carved in the form of the scarab, or dung beetle. The dung beetle lays its eggs inside balls of animal droppings. When the eggs hatch, the balls break apart and dozens of baby beetles run out. The ancient Egyptians saw this and thought that the scarab created new life by magic. It became their symbol of rebirth and was worshipped as the rising sun which begins each new day. Especially important was the heart scarab, which was inscribed with a magic spell to prevent a dead person's heart from revealing their bad deeds when it was weighed in the court of Osiris. Part of it reads:

O my heart which I had from my mother! Do not stand up as a witness against me in the judgement hall ... do not tell them what I have really done!
Book of the Dead, Spell 30B

Heart scarabs.

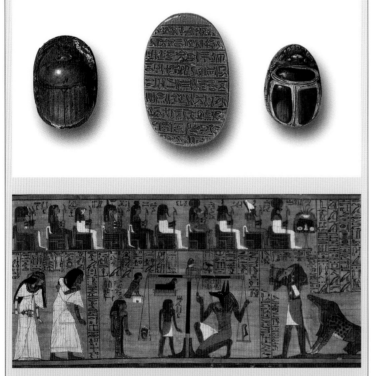

Page from a Book of the Dead, showing Anubis weighing the heart in the court of Osiris. If the heart of the dead person weighed more than the feather of truth, it was eaten by the monster on the right.

shabtis

Another important item of funeral equipment was a small, magic figure called a shabti or ushabti, which means 'answerer'. If the god Osiris, who ruled the underworld, asked a dead person to work in The Field of Reeds, the shabti would do the work instead. Some shabtis carry a hoe for digging in the fields and a flail for threshing grain. Important people such as kings often had huge numbers of shabtis. For example, Tutankhamun had 365 worker shabtis – one for each day of the year – and 48 overseer shabtis to supervize them.

Shabtis were usually inscribed with a magic spell which said:

O shabti allotted to me, if I am called or if I am detailed to do any work that has to be done in the realm of the dead ... you shall offer yourself for me on every occasion of cultivating the fields, flooding the banks or moving sand from east to west. 'Here I am!' you shall say.
Book of the Dead, Spell 6

Shabtis.

When someone wealthy died, the body was taken to the embalmers for mummification, which normally took 70 days. During this time, the dead person's family was in mourning. To show their sorrow, they shaved off their eyebrows, put dirt on their heads and wore torn clothes. They would also be busy gathering all the offerings for the tomb and making preparations for the funeral. When everything was ready, the dead person's mummy was taken to the tomb in a procession. If the deceased had been wealthy, the body would be taken on a sledge drawn by bulls, and professional mourners would accompany the procession, weeping and wailing. When they reached the tomb, there was a special ceremony called the Opening of the Mouth, which was meant to restore the dead person's senses for life in the next world. The instructions for the funeral rites were written down in special texts known as Spells for Coming Forth by Day, which we now call the Book of the Dead. Copies of these texts were also placed in tombs for the dead to use as guidebooks to the afterlife.

THE VALLEY OF THE KINGS

The Valley of the Kings, seen from the air. The dark spots near the valley floor are the entrances to royal tombs.

Throughout the New Kingdom (1550 to 1069 BC), Egypt's rulers were buried in the Valley of the Kings, a remote valley hidden in the desert mountains west of Thebes. Most of the tombs in the Valley of the Kings consist of a long tunnel going deep into the earth and ending in a burial chamber, where the king's mummy was laid to rest in a massive stone sarcophagus. Small rooms around the chamber held the offerings the king would need for the afterlife. The walls and ceilings of the chamber were covered with paintings of gods and goddesses meant to help the king on his journey through the underworld.

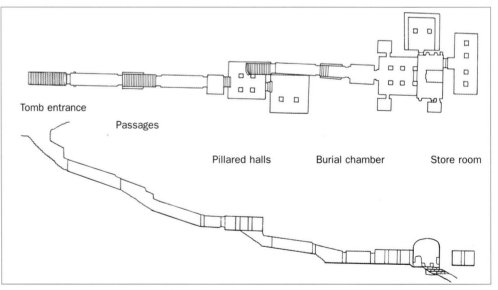

Plan and section of the tomb of Sety I in the Valley of the Kings.

Digging out a royal tomb took many years. One of the first things a new king did when he came to the throne was to order the preparation of his tomb. Once a site had been chosen, digging was started. The tomb builders used methods learned from stone quarrying. They worked in two teams, one team on the left side of the tomb, and the other on the right. Each member of the team had a special job. The first to start work were the excavators, who cut out the rough shape of the monument. They were followed by the masons, who smoothed the walls and shaped the columns that supported the roof. Last of all came the sculptors and artists who decorated the walls.

The paintings were done by a team of artists. Strict rules controlled the proportions of important parts of

Painting in the tomb of Tutankhamun.

Howard Carter with Tutankhamun's mummy.

Cutaway view of Tutankhamun's tomb.

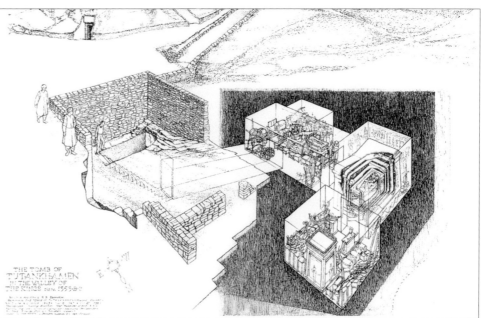

the paintings. Some paintings were started with the aid of a square grid. After the chief draughtsman had checked and corrected each drawing, the outlines were filled in with colour. More skilled artists completed the details, and the chief added the finishing touches after checking the work again.

Like other people, kings were buried with everything they needed for the next life, but their belongings were especially magnificent and valuable. Because they were gods, their bodies were protected by masks and coffins made of solid gold, and amulets made of precious stones. Although robbing a royal tomb was a terrible crime punishable by death, these treasures were a powerful temptation to thieves. At first, the entrances to the tombs were disguised to deter tomb robbers, but the cemetery officials soon stopped trying to conceal them and relied on

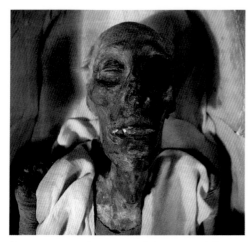

The unwrapped mummy of Rameses II from his tomb in the Valley of the Kings.

security guards instead. Despite these precautions, nearly all the tombs were robbed in ancient times.

Of the 62 tombs which have been discovered in the Valley of the Kings, only the tomb of Tutankhamun was found intact. It was preserved because a later tomb had been built above it and the rock which the builders dug out covered it. Tutankhamun had not been king for long. Memory of him soon faded and before long nobody remembered that he was buried there. Even his name was forgotten. It was not until the British archaeologist Howard Carter found some objects with Tutankhamun's name on them in the Valley of the Kings that anyone suspected the existence of the tomb. Carter searched carefully, and was rewarded in 1922 when he

discovered some steps leading down to a sealed tomb. Inside, Tutankhamun still lay in his solid gold coffin, surrounded by all his treasures. Today, the young king that everyone forgot is perhaps Egypt's most famous pharaoh.

Above: Gold funeral mask of Tutankhamun.

DEIR EL-MEDINA

Deir el-Medina

Digging out the tombs and making the funeral goods for royal burials required an army of workers and provided many jobs for local people. Early in the New Kingdom, the government decided to build a special village to house the artists and craftsmen who

Anherkau and his son lived at Deir el-Medina.

Tomb at Deir el-Medina.

Above: Burial chamber in the tomb of Sennedjem at Deir el-Medina. The painting shows Sennedjem and his wife at work in the Fields of Reeds in the next life.

Below: Work registers like this recorded which villagers were absent from their work, and why.

worked on the royal tombs in the Valley of the Kings and the Valley of the Queens. They chose a site in a desert valley, among the cemeteries on the Nile's west bank. Today, this village is called Deir el-Medina.

Because Deir el-Medina was so far from other villages, the workmen's wives and children had to live there, too. So, over the years, the village became a real community, with up to 70 families living there at one time. The village was completely self-contained. Its remote location meant that everything the villagers needed had to be brought to them, including

their clothes, food and drinking water. They even had their own temples to worship the gods, and when they died they were buried in tombs cut into the side of the valley.

Deir el-Medina remained in use for almost 400 years. Then, at the end of the New Kingdom (about 1069 BC), attacks by Libyan bandits made life in the isolated village too dangerous and it was abandoned. The villagers left behind their homes and temples, their ancestors' tombs and thousands of documents, including letters, poems, stories, work and court records, cartoons

Above: Reconstruction of the village at Deir el-Medina and its cemetery.

Below: A workman's house at Deir el-Medina.

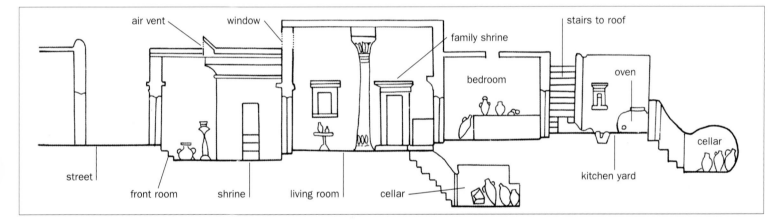

and sketches, even laundry lists. Nothing was built there afterwards, so the village is very well preserved, helping archaeologists to understand how ordinary Egyptians lived during the New Kingdom.

The houses at Deir el-Medina were built side by side along the village's narrow main street. Most ancient Egyptian houses were made completely of mud brick. Because Deir el-Medina was in the desert, the lower levels were built of stone plastered with mud. A wooden front door led into a small front room containing a shrine and leading to a larger main room. The main room had a wooden column in the middle to support a high ceiling made of palm logs. Close to the ceiling tiny windows let in the light, and air vents on the roof allowed cool breezes to blow through the house.

Stairs led up to the roof, which provided storage space and a place to work in the daytime. In hot weather, the family could sleep there at night. At the back of the house was a small kitchen yard with a stone for grinding grain and a clay oven for baking.

Like most ancient Egyptian homes, these houses had very little furniture. Around the walls of the main room there were mud benches

Furniture from an ancient Egyptian home.

where people sat during the day and slept at night. The family's clothes and belongings were stored in wooden chests or pottery jars. Nearly all the houses had cellars where valuables could be stored in safety.

SPOTLIGHT ON ASWAN

Aswan .

The modern city of Aswan, in southern Egypt, is built around the first Nile cataract. Here, islands of granite block the river, making it impassable to boats. In ancient times, this natural barrier formed Egypt's southern frontier, and the town grew up around the garrison stationed on the island of Elephantine to protect the border. Later, Aswan's granite quarries became an important source of stone for buildings, royal statues and sarcophagi.

The ancient Egyptian name for Elephantine was *abu*, which means 'elephant'. It may have got this name because the big, grey rocks of the cataract look like elephants bathing in the water. Or perhaps it was because

The Nile at Aswan.

the town was an important trading centre for ivory and other exotic African products, such as gold, incense and wild animals. Aswan's modern name probably comes from another ancient Egyptian word, *swenet*, which means 'market'.

The ancient governors of Aswan became very rich from the African trade, and built themselves beautiful rock tombs high in the sandstone cliffs of the Nile's west bank. One of the most interesting tombs there belonged to an army general called Harkhuf, whose tomb inscription describes how he led three African trading expeditions.

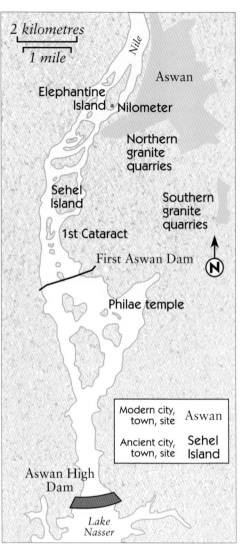

Map of Aswan.

Sarenput II was a governor of Aswan during the Middle Kingdom.

The god Khnum.

A CLOSER LOOK AT... # Philae

The Temple of Isis at Philae.

In Greek and Roman times the temple of Isis at Philae, just south of Aswan, was one of the most important pilgrimage centres of Egypt. It was built on an island in the middle of the Nile, close to another island where there was a shrine to Osiris, the husband of Isis. Isis was the goddess of magic, and the ancient Egyptians believed that her temple would give magical protection to Egypt's southern border. Philae was the last of Egypt's temples to remain in use. People worshipped there until the 6th century AD. After the Aswan High Dam was built, Philae was often flooded, so in the 1970s, the whole temple was taken apart, like a giant jigsaw puzzle, and moved to a safe place on another island nearby.

Aswan was also important to the ancient Egyptians as the mythological source of the Nile flood, which they thought flowed from a cave under the cataract. Many temples were built to please the local deities Khnum and Satet, so that they would deliver the annual flood on which Egypt's farmers depended to grow their crops. The rocks of the cataract are covered with royal names and inscriptions.

As soon as the Nile waters began to rise each year, officials started to check its height using the Nilometer on Elephantine Island. The Nilometer was a series of stone steps going down into the river. By watching how long it took the water to cover the steps, the officials could work out how fast the Nile was rising and how high it was likely to get.

Left: Rock inscriptions at Sahel Island.

Right: The Nilometer on Elephantine Island.

QUARRYING AND BUILDING

Most ancient Egyptian buildings were made of organic materials – wood, reeds, and mud – but for tombs and temples, which were meant to last forever, stone was used. The Egyptians used many different kinds of stone for building, but the most important were limestone, found in the north of Egypt, and sandstone, found in the south. To save transportation time, stone was usually quarried as close to the building site as possible, but good quality stone sometimes had to come from further away.

The most important limestone quarry was at Tura, near Cairo, which provided the fine limestone used to cover the Old Kingdom pyramids. The best sandstone came from Gebel el-Silsila, near Edfu, and was used to build many of the temples in the south of Egypt. Shrines, doorways and temple columns were often made from the precious black and red granite quarried at Aswan.

Limestone and sandstone were quarried using bronze tools, but granite is much harder and had to be quarried using hammers made of hard rock. The stone could then be worked into shape with metal chisels or round hammer stones. Large objects, such as obelisks, statues and sarcophagi, were often roughly shaped in the rock before they were cut free from it. Once it had been quarried, the stone was loaded on to barges and taken to its destination by water.

Most building work was probably done during the Nile flood, when farmworkers were free to help and the high water made it easier to bring the barges loaded with stone close to the building site. Egyptian buildings did not have deep foundations sunk into the ground. Instead, the ground to be built on was levelled and made firm. Once this was done, the stone blocks were roughly shaped before being dragged into position using sledges on rollers.

An unfinished sculpture of a queen or goddess.

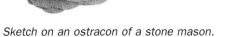

Sketch on an ostracon of a stone mason.

An Egyptian mason's mallet.

An unfinished colonnade and the remains of a builders' ramp at Karnak.

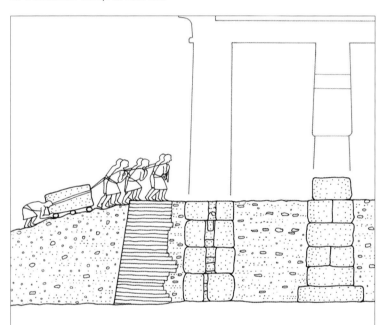

How a ramp was used to build a colonnade like the one above.

No mortar was used to hold the stones together, so their surfaces had to fit really well.

As a building grew higher, mud brick ramps were constructed to raise the stones to the upper levels. When the structure was complete, the stones were smoothed and carved from the top down, as the ramps were taken away. Finally, the carved reliefs were plastered and painted. Many buildings were never finished, which has proved very useful for archaeologists, who have used them to work out how Egyptian buildings were constructed.

A CLOSER LOOK AT...

obelisks

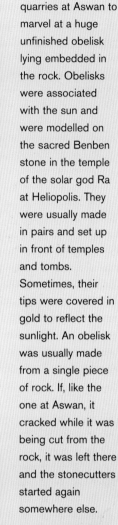

Every year, thousands of visitors are attracted to the quarries at Aswan to marvel at a huge unfinished obelisk lying embedded in the rock. Obelisks were associated with the sun and were modelled on the sacred Benben stone in the temple of the solar god Ra at Heliopolis. They were usually made in pairs and set up in front of temples and tombs. Sometimes, their tips were covered in gold to reflect the sunlight. An obelisk was usually made from a single piece of rock. If, like the one at Aswan, it cracked while it was being cut from the rock, it was left there and the stonecutters started again somewhere else.

This obelisk from Karnak temple was quarried at Aswan.

An unfinished obelisk in the northern granite quarry at Aswan. This obelisk was abandoned when the stone cracked.

THE DESERT AND OASES

Desert landscape.

The ancient Egyptians regarded the desert as a wild and dangerous place, quite different from the fertile lands of the Nile which gave life to Egypt. In contrast, the desert was a place of death, a wasteland where travellers who lost their way died of thirst and hunger under the blazing sun. It was the place where the dead were buried, and its scrublands were home to dangerous animals, such as lions and wild bulls. The advantage of this inhospitable environment was that it protected Egypt's borders, making it almost impossible for an enemy to attack from the east or west.

Seth, the god of the desert, represented everything the Egyptians most feared. He was the god of chaos, storms and warfare, the murderer of Osiris and the eternal enemy of Horus. Kings of Egypt often hunted desert animals as a way of showing their superior power over Seth and his creatures.

But the desert also held many of Egypt's most precious resources. The mountains between the Nile and the Red Sea were rich in valuable minerals, gold and metal ores, such as copper, lead and tin. The Wadi Natrun, a desert valley to the west of the Nile Delta, was the main source of natron, which was used to make glass and glazes, in mummification, and as a detergent.

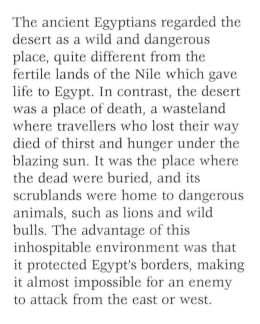

Left: An Egyptian official worships the god Seth.

Below: King Rameses III hunting wild bulls.

Above: This scarab of King Amenhotep III records how he hunted lions in the desert.

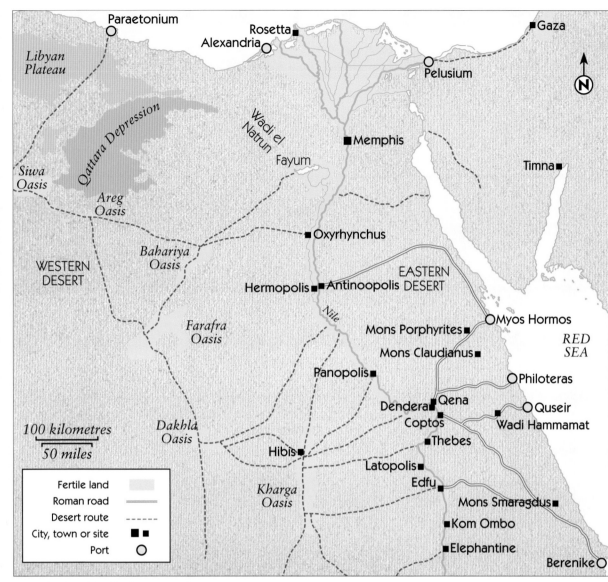

Map showing Egypt's deserts and oases.

Goats grazing at an oasis near a desert spring.

Not all of the desert was arid. The scrublands along the fringes of the Nile Valley provided grazing for herds of sheep and goats tended by nomadic tribes. These herders maintained a lifestyle that had existed before the first Egyptians settled the Nile Valley and Delta. The Egyptians called these people the Travellers on the Sands. Today, they are known as Bedouin. Many Bedouin still live in Egypt's eastern desert, and especially in the Sinai Peninsula. Some have settled in towns, but many still follow their traditional way of life, travelling the deserts with their flocks and living in large black tents of woven goat hair.

As well as scrublands, there are oases in the deserts. An oasis is a place where underground water comes to the surface, making it possible for people to live and grow food there. Most of the oases in Egypt are in the desert west of the Nile. In ancient times the largest ones were like country towns, with public buildings, temples and cemeteries.

In ancient times, the oases played an important role in Egypt's trading network as stopping places for traders crossing the desert. The only safe way to reach the oases was to join a caravan, an organized expedition of people and pack animals who travelled together for protection. People who disagreed with the government were sometimes sent to live in the oases, because they were so isolated. There they could not cause so much trouble and would find it very difficult to escape.

Siwa town.

SPOTLIGHT ON
SINAI
AND THE EASTERN DESERT

St Catherine's monastery in Sinai is one of the oldest monasteries in Egypt.

The deserts east of the Nile were Egypt's principal source of metal ores and precious gemstones, but the hostile desert environment made mining and transporting them a difficult task. The mountains were deep in the desert and the only way there was on foot or by donkey. Water was scarce and many expeditions had to turn back before everyone died of thirst. Eventually, wells were dug to allow miners to work in remote areas. Carved inscriptions at the mines record the dates of mining expeditions, and sometimes the names of the miners.

Among the gemstones mined in the Eastern Desert were purple amethysts, green beryls and emeralds, orange-red or green jasper and red carnelian, and clear quartz crystal. Turquoise was mined in Sinai. The turquoise mines were sacred to the love goddess Hathor, who was worshipped there as the Lady of Turquoise. All these gemstones were prized for making jewellery and for decorating furniture and royal statues. In Roman times, building stones, such

Reconstruction of an ancient mine in the Eastern Desert.

Mountains in the Eastern Desert.

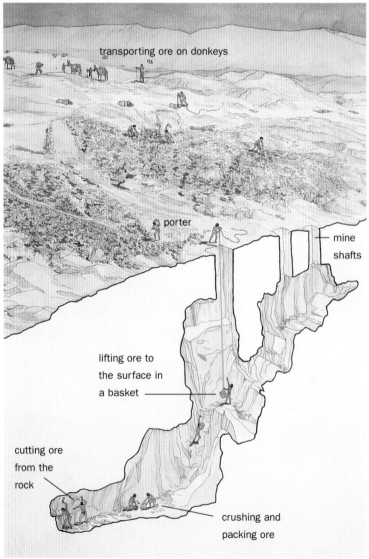

transporting ore on donkeys

porter

mine shafts

lifting ore to the surface in a basket

cutting ore from the rock

crushing and packing ore

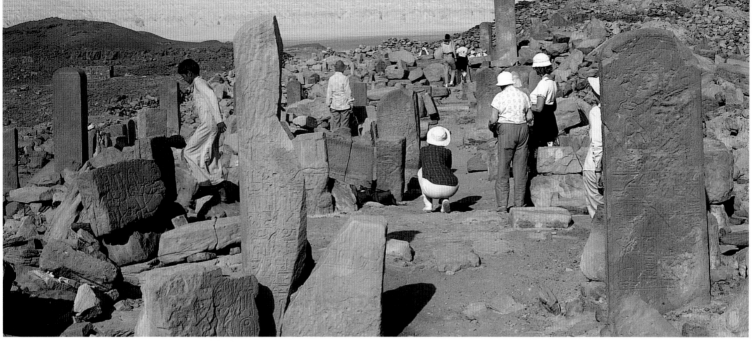

Tourists visiting the Temple of Hathor at Serabit el-Khadim in Sinai.

as granite and porphyry, were mined in the Eastern Desert. Convicted criminals were sometimes sent to the mines as forced labour.

Prospecting and mining expeditions were the job of the army. Prospecting for gemstones and metal ores was a difficult job. It required an expert eye to spot the veins of minerals hidden within the mountains. But this was only the beginning. Once a promising vein had been identified, the gemstone or ore had to be extracted. The gold

The goddess Hathor.

deposits in the Eastern Desert lay within veins of quartz rock, which had to be hacked out, crushed, and then washed to extract the gold. The gold, in the form of dust, nuggets, or roughly-worked rings, was carried back to the cities of the Nile Valley on the backs of porters or donkeys.

Like gold, copper was known and worked in Egypt from prehistoric times. Copper does occur naturally in its metallic form, and this was how the Egyptians first discovered it. More often, however, it is found as an ore which has to be smelted to produce the metal (see page 22). One of the first metals the early Egyptians learned to smelt was copper. Most of Egypt's copper was mined in Sinai and smelted on the spot before it was transported to the Nile Valley.

The valleys of the Eastern Desert also played an important role in trading, providing routes between the Nile Valley and the Red Sea. In the Late Period (747 to 332 BC), a canal was dug to provide a direct link between the Nile and the Red Sea. Sinai was the link between Egypt and the lands to the north and west, and a major trading route. However, it was also vulnerable to invaders and so was heavily protected with well-guarded forts.

Green jasper and gold heart scarab.

Amulets made of blue turquoise and red jasper. They were placed on mummies for magical protection.

SPOTLIGHT ON THE WESTERN DESERT AND ITS OASES

Western Desert

Egypt's Western Desert formed a natural barrier between Egypt and Libya. However, the ancient Egyptians were always alert to the danger of invasion and guarded as much of the region as possible.

The Western Desert is not as rich in resources as the Eastern Desert. There are no minerals apart from the natron deposits, in the Wadi Natrun, and alum, (used in dyeing cloth), in Kharga Oasis. However, some of the desert oases became trading and frontier posts. The five most important oases were Kharga, Dakhla, Farafra, Bahariya and Siwa. All of them were inhabited from prehistoric times, and those closest to the Nile were probably under Egyptian control from the Old Kingdom (2686 to 2182 BC) onwards.

Tomb painting of a vineyard, with workers picking grapes and pressing them into wine.

Below: The Temple of Hibis at Kharga Oasis.

Above: Sand dunes in the Western Desert.

Date palm tree.

The western oases were formed by wind erosion scooping out depressions in the desert. Because these areas are lower than the surrounding land, they are closer to the underlying water table, allowing the water to rise to the surface as springs. The inhabitants of the oases soon discovered that they could also access this water by digging wells. These water supplies made it possible for them to grow food, and the oases became famous for their dates and wine.

The ruins of the temple of Amun at Siwa Oasis.

Mummies in the Roman cemetery at Bahariya.

questions. In the 6th century BC, the Persian king Cambyses was supposed to have sent an army to capture Siwa and destroy the temple of Amun, but his soldiers vanished in the desert before they reached the oasis. The Egyptians believed that Amun had sent a sandstorm to kill the Persian invaders.

When Alexander the Great arrived in Egypt in 332 BC, one of the first things he did was to make the dangerous journey across the desert to Siwa to worship at the Temple of Amun and consult the oracle there. The temple priests greeted Alexander as the son of Amun, confirming him as the rightful ruler of Egypt.

Coin showing Alexander the Great wearing the ram's horns of the god Amun.

Many of the remains in the oasis towns date from the Roman period (30 BC to AD 395). In 2000, a large cemetery containing Roman mummies was discovered at Bahariya. The mummies had been wonderfully preserved by the dry desert sand, and many had beautiful golden masks. New discoveries are still being made in what is now called the Valley of the Golden Mummies.

Siwa is the largest and most westerly of Egypt's oases, and did not come under Egyptian control

until the Late Period (747 to 332 BC). Siwa is still difficult to reach, but in ancient times getting there from the Nile Valley took at least three weeks. Siwa is located close to Egypt's border with Libya, and its people are related to the Berbers of North Africa. Even today, they speak a different language from the Egyptians.

Siwa was a sacred place both for the Libyans and for the Egyptians, and was famous throughout the Mediterranean world for its temple oracle – a mysterious statue of the god Amun which answered people's

PART FOUR
THE STUDY OF EGYPT

REDISCOVERING ANCIENT EGYPT

People have always been fascinated by Ancient Egypt. Until Egyptologists learned to decipher ancient Egyptian scripts in the early 19th century, they got their ideas about ancient Egypt from the Bible and from what the Greeks and Romans had written about it. In the past, all well-educated people could read Greek and Latin, and sometimes Hebrew, too. By the 17th century, those who did not understand these languages could read translations of the Bible and of books by classical writers. Ancient travellers, such as Herodotus, wrote long accounts of their journeys in Egypt, in which they tried to make sense of all the stories which they had heard and the strange things which they had seen. Although they are not always accurate, these books are still important sources of information about ancient Egypt.

During medieval times, many of these books were studied and translated by the Arab scholars who lived in Cairo, and foreign visitors still came to wonder at the ancient monuments. Egypt was still an important centre of trade, and it controlled the sea route between Europe and India. Many countries wanted to be able to control this trade for themselves. In AD 1517, Egypt was conquered by Turkey, and became a part of the Ottoman Empire.

In 1798, a French army led by Napoleon challenged the Ottomans by invading Egypt and occupying it. Napoleon's army included a team of scholars, including artists and engineers, who were set to work making a survey of all the ancient monuments in Egypt. Their work went on for four years and was published between 1809 and 1822,

The Battle of the Nile.

Napoleon Bonaparte.

Horatio Nelson.

as the *Description de l'Egypte* (Description of Egypt), in 24 volumes. This was the first systematic study of ancient Egyptian monuments ever made.

Meanwhile, France and Britain were at war, and the British agreed to help the Ottomans to expel the

French from Egypt. In August 1798, the British fleet, commanded by Admiral Nelson, won the Battle of the Nile, a great sea battle fought off the Egyptian coast. After the defeat of Napoleon's army, many of the ancient Egyptian objects the French had collected were surrendered to the British and shipped to England.

Among them was the famous Rosetta Stone, which had been discovered by one of Napoleon's soldiers in 1799 at the village of Rosetta in the Nile Delta.

The stone was inscribed with a decree of King Ptolemy V written in 196 BC. What made the discovery so exciting was that the decree was written in three different scripts. The first two versions were in ancient Egyptian, written in hieroglyphs and Demotic. The third version was in Greek. Because the Greek script could be read, it provided clues to understanding the Egyptian writing.

The Rosetta Stone was taken to London and eventually placed in the British Museum in 1802. Copies of its inscription were sent to scholars around the world. In 1822 a Frenchman, Jean François Champollion, announced that, using the Rosetta Stone, he had deciphered hieroglyphs. This brilliant breakthrough finally made it possible for the ancient Egyptian language to be understood.

The Rosetta Stone.

Left: Scholars looking at the Rosetta Stone in the British Museum.

Jean François Champollion.

MODERN EGYPT

People who resisted British rule were treated harshly and their leaders were killed, put in prison or forced to leave Egypt.

After the French were expelled from Egypt, Egypt was restored to the Ottoman Empire, but a new ruling family came to power. The first of these rulers, Muhammad Ali Pasha, was determined to turn Egypt into a modern European-style country. He introduced new crops, such as cotton and sugar cane, and re-established Alexandria as a major Mediterranean port. In 1856, his son, Said Pasha, gave a French company permission to built the Suez Canal linking the Mediterranean to the Red Sea. The canal, which opened in 1869, created a direct sea route between Europe and India, saving merchants a vast amount of time and money. Before this, ships bound for India and other Far Eastern countries had to sail all the way round Africa.

In the 19th and early 20th centuries Egypt became a popular destination for European tourists.

Much of what the British did was for their own benefit, not to help the Egyptians. However, new roads and railways were built and the Nile irrigation systems were improved to help farmers grow more crops. The British encouraged the Egyptian farmers to grow cotton for British textile manufacturers. But when Egyptians tried to start their own textile factories, the British stopped them. All the best jobs in the government were held by the British, and foreigners had more rights in law than Egyptians did.

Muhammad Ali.

In 1875, Muhammad Ali's grandson, Khedive Ismail, was forced to sell to Britain 40 per cent of his shares in the Suez Canal company. This gave Britain an excuse to send troops to Egypt and guard the canal. In 1876, Egypt was bankrupt, which led to Britain and France taking control of Egyptian finances in order to protect European investments. This was followed by a nationalist uprising in 1881, which resulted in British occupation of Egypt. Officially, the Khedive was still the ruler, but Britain really controlled what happened in Egypt.

Because of the Suez Canal, Egypt played an important strategic role in World Wars I and II. At the beginning of World War I, Turkey sided with Germany. This gave the British the excuse to seize Egypt and declare it a British Protectorate. There was still an Egyptian ruler, but he had no real power.

After the war, there were more and more demands for Egyptian independence. In 1922, Britain ended the Protectorate and Egypt became independent, with some conditions. The British insisted on their right to defend the Suez Canal, so British troops remained in Egypt. After the outbreak of World War II in 1939, Egypt was invaded in 1940 by Italian forces. In 1941 the German Afrika Korps joined them. Having pushed halfway across Egypt, they were defeated by British and Commonwealth troops at the Battle of el-Alamein in October 1942. The war ended in 1945 and the British finally left Egypt in 1947, except for the Suez Canal zone.

In 1952 a group of army officers overthrew the Egyptian king Faruk, forcing him into exile. In 1953 Egypt became a republic. By 1955, plans had been made to build a new high dam across the Nile at Aswan. The USA had offered financial aid for this project, but withdrew its

The Suez Canal.

offer in 1956 after Egypt recognized the Republic of China, a Communist state.

In 1956 Gamal Abdul Nasser became President of Egypt. In the same year he nationalized the Suez Canal to raise money to build a new dam across the Nile at Aswan to control the annual Nile floods. In response Britain, Israel and France invaded Egypt, but the United Nations condemned the action and they were forced to withdraw.

President Nasser.

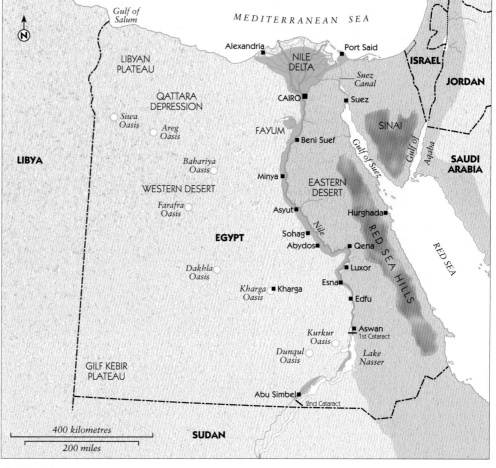

Modern Egypt.

The state of Israel was created in 1943 from land that had formerly been part of Palestine. Many of the neighbouring Arab states, including Egypt, were strongly opposed to this, and as a result there has been a great deal of conflict in the region. In 1967, Egypt blockaded the Israeli port of Eilat. In retaliation Israel invaded Egypt and occupied the Sinai peninsula. In 1973, Egypt and Syria attacked Israel, and Egypt regained some of the lost territory, but not all of it. The conflict was ended by the United Nations, and in 1979 Egypt and Israel signed a peace treaty. By 1982, the Sinai peninsula had been restored to Egypt.

The first dam at Aswan had been built by the British and completed in 1902. It helped to control the Nile flood but it was only partly effective. The new Aswan High Dam was started in 1960 and completed in the 1970s with help from Russia. Now, instead of flooding Egypt, the Nile inundation is held back behind the dam,

The hydroelectric plant at the Aswan dam.

creating a huge artificial lake called Lake Nasser. The waters of Lake Nasser now cover the land that used to be Nubia. All the people who lived there had to be moved to new villages. Some important Nubian archaeological sites, such as the temples at Abu Simbel, were moved to higher ground but other sites disappeared beneath the waters.

Controlling the water stored in Lake Nasser has made possible the irrigation of 405,000 hectares (1 million acres) of new farmland where crops can be grown all year

Policemen protect the ancient sites of Egypt and the tourists who visit them.

round. The hydroelectric turbines in the dam generate 10 billion kilowatt-hours of electric power every year. But watering the farmland continuously is causing the level of ground water to rise, damaging the ancient monuments. In the Delta, this high water table allows salt from the sea to soak into the land, making it harder to cultivate crops. Many people are worried that the rise in sea level caused by global warming will make this problem worse in future.

THE STUDY OF EGYPT

After Napoleon's scholars had published their survey and Champollion had published his discoveries, scholars and antiquarians began taking a serious interest in the study of ancient Egypt. Egypt had become a magnet for treasure hunters, and although many sites were discovered and excavated at this time, most of the excavators were interested only in getting objects to sell. Things which could not be sold were often thrown away.

Realising how much vital information was being lost forever, a new generation of Egyptologists, such as the American George Reisner (1867–1942) and the Englishman William Flinders Petrie (1853–1942), began to develop systematic excavation and recording techniques. They understood that knowing where things were found, how they were placed together and how deep they were buried provided important clues for building up an accurate picture of how the ancient Egyptians lived and died. The methods they pioneered formed the basis of modern Egyptology.

Many of the objects collected in Egypt during the 19th century found their way into museums around the world, such as the British Museum in London, the Musée du Louvre in Paris and the Metropolitan Museum of Art in New York. In 1858, the Frenchman Auguste Mariette (1821–81) started putting together the greatest collection of all, the Egyptian Museum in Cairo. This houses some of the most famous ancient Egyptian objects ever found, including the treasures of Tutankhamun, excavated from his tomb in the Valley of the Kings by Howard Carter (1874–1939) in 1922.

An early study expedition to Thebes led by Bernardino Drovetti, the French consul in Egypt.

Above: An enormous bust of Rameses II being moved in 1816.

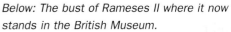

Below: The bust of Rameses II where it now stands in the British Museum.

The Egyptian Museum in Cairo.

Today the Egyptian Museum and all the archaeological sites of Egypt are cared for by the Supreme Council of Antiquities, a department of the Egyptian government.

One of their most important jobs has been to prevent anyone from illegally taking antiquities out of Egypt. Another has been saving the Nubian monuments that were flooded when the Aswan High Dam was built. Two of the most important buildings were the rock-cut temples of Ramesses II at Abu Simbel. In the 1960s, with help from UNESCO, these were taken apart, moved and put back together on higher ground above the level of Lake Nasser.

Although Egyptologists still excavate ancient Egyptian sites using traditional techniques, science has given them many new tools. Aerial photography can help with the surveying of sites. Computers can be used to keep excavation records

The locations of Egyptian collections in museums around the world.

The operation to rescue the temples of Abu Simbel from Lake Nasser.

Above: An archaeologist carefully records an ancient Egyptian burial.

and process information. Medical techniques, such as X-rays, CAT scanning and DNA testing, have been used on mummies to learn about sickness and health in ancient Egypt. The chemical analysis of materials can help to reveal the sources of objects and how they were made.

Egyptologists have many different kinds of jobs. They may work as field archaeologists, epigraphers (people who copy and study inscriptions), philologists and linguists (people who study ancient writing and languages), scientific researchers, museum curators, papyrologists (people who study papyri), writers, teachers, illustrators or conservators. What they all have in common is that they are working together to extend our knowledge of ancient Egypt.

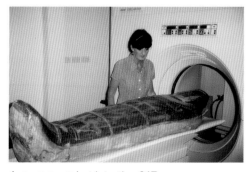

A mummy going into the CAT scanner – a special kind of X-ray that allows us to see inside the mummy without damaging it.

Egyptian antiquities still inspire enthusiastic interest in people around the world.

Index

Glossary

Amulets
Protective charms.

Book of the Dead
A collection of magic spells written on papyrus and placed in the tomb to protect the dead in the afterlife.

Canopic jars
A set of four containers for the internal organs of a mummy.

Cartouche
A protective oval ring surrounding a royal name. The cartouche is a longer form of the *shen* hieroglyph, meaning 'eternity'.

Catacombs
Underground rooms used for burials.

Cataracts
Rocky outcrops in a riverbed that create rapids or waterfalls, making the river impassable to boats. The first Nile cataract, at modern Aswan, marked Egypt's southern boundary.

Cenotaph
A symbolic, empty, tomb.

Delta
Triangular area of flat land created when a river spreads out before entering the sea.

Dynasty
A family of rulers.

False door
A dummy entrance, usually in a tomb, that allowed the spirits of the dead to come and go.

Hypostyle hall
A columned hall in a temple.

Inundation
The annual Nile flood.

Khedive
Title of the Ottoman governor of Egypt.

Mastaba
A low, rectangular tomb with an underground burial chamber.

Natron
A natural salt used in mummification and glassmaking, and as a detergent and disinfectant.

Pasha
Title of a high official in the Ottoman empire.

Pharaoh
Greek translation of *per-aa*, meaning 'Great House'. From the New Kingdom onwards 'Pharaoh' became a way of referring to the king.

Pylon
The monumental entrance to an Egyptian temple.

Scarab
A beetle-shaped amulet.

Shabti
A small servant figure placed in the tomb to serve the dead in the afterlife. Sometimes also called a *ushabti.*

Shaduf
A device used to raise water from the Nile to irrigate fields.

Sons of Horus
Four gods who protected a mummy's internal organs.

Stela
An inscribed commemorative panel, usually made of stone.

Wadi
A dry desert riverbed that occasionally floods during heavy rainfall.